Rivers of Glory

Flowing Down to the Soul of a Wounded Generation

Sandy Davis Kirk, Ph.D.

Unless otherwise noted, all Scripture references are from the New International Version of the Bible, copyright © 1973, 1978, 1984 by International Bible Society, Colorado Springs, Colorado. References marked KJV are from the Authorized King James Version of the Bible. References marked NKJ are from the New King James Version of the Bible, copyright © 1979, 1980, 1982 by Thomas Nelson, Inc., Nashville, Tennessee. References marked AMP are from The Amplified Bible, copyright © 1987 by The Lockman Foundation, La Habra, California. References marked MT are from the Masoretic Text, copyright © 1955 by the Jewish Publication Society, Philadelphia, Pennsylvania.

McDougal Publishing is a ministry of The McDougal Foundation, Inc., a Maryland nonprofit corporation dedicated to spreading the Gospel of the Lord Jesus Christ to as many people as possible in the shortest time possible.

Published by:
McDougal Publishing
P.O. Box 3595
Hagerstown, MD 21742-3595
www.mcdougalpublishing.com

ISBN 1-58158-093-2

Printed in the United States of America
For Worldwide Distribution
Front Cover Photos by Ray Hayes, www.raysphotos.net

Dedication

This book is dedicated to a young generation, especially to my three most precious treasures on earth — Lance, Misti, and Christi.

Contents

The Cry:

For because He Himself [in His humanity] *has suffered in being tempted (tested and tried), He is able* [immediately] *to run to the cry of (assist, relieve) those who are being tempted* and *tested* and *tried* [and who therefore are being exposed to suffering].

Hebrews 2:18, AMP

The Answer:

If anyone is thirsty, let him come to me and drink...and out of his innermost being will flow rivers.

John 7:37-38

Chosen for the River
Come Drink From Rivers of Revival

"Friends, it's a literal river! You can feel it. You can actually feel the current of it!" cried Pastor John Kilpatrick when revival swelled to flood stage at his church in Pensacola.[1] Even today, over ten years later, God's river flows down from Heaven to a new generation.

Listen....Can you hear it? Can you feel the raw power of the river of God roaring closer? Come hold your thirsty heart beneath the flooding streams of this river. Drink in the goodness and let His glory flood over you.

If you have pain inside, come soak the ache in your soul in these healing currents until the hurt floats away like logs on a mountain stream. Keep on drinking until you can hold no more. Then let these living waters spill out to your whole generation.

In these pages, you'll read stories of young men and women who are moving with God in this river. The purpose of these stories is to help you see how you can leap into the floods yourself.

For a new breed of young ministers has come of age on planet earth. One burning passion consumes them. They've been gripped by looking long and deep at the Pierced One on the cross. They've drunk deeply of the river flowing down from the Lamb until their hearts burn to bring Him the reward of His suffering.

Driven by this pure motive, their hearts bleed for lost souls, ache for the poor, and yearn to bring living water to thirsty ones. They would rather wipe the tears of prostitutes and feed the bellies of orphans than climb corporate ladders in the world or political ladders in the church.

So come to the waters and drink. Stand in the midst of these rushing streams and look up at the source of this river. Gaze up at the Lamb upon the throne until He fills you with rivers of fresh wine. For God has chosen a young generation, and all who are still young at heart,[2] as the wineskin for this new wine.

Whether you are old or young, let's all come like little children. Let's humble ourselves and dive into the cooling streams, splashing like kids in a summer pool. Come now and behold the Lamb until He fills you to overflowing with *Rivers of Glory*.

Endnotes:
   1. John Kilpatrick, "Intercessors' Service," Brownsville Assembly of God, Pensacola, FL, 1996.
   2. **Note to those over forty:** Let me say a word about the huge differences in the generations, for we were the modern generation; those under forty are a postmodern generation. Our faith was based on reason; theirs is based on experience. Ours was a productive generation; theirs is a relational generation. We were success driven;

they are love driven. "Time is money," we said; they say, "Time is hangin' out with someone who cares." We often climbed the ladder and left our children down below. Now they long for a hand to reach down and lift them alongside. It's not a rung on the ladder they want; it's a relationship with someone who cares. They yearn for mentors who will take the time to show them real love.

Though I write this book to the young, I think it will help those who are older to understand the pain and passion of a young generation. So if you're over forty, won't you join me in this God-breathed opportunity to mentor a deeply wounded generation? Let's humble ourselves like little children, release the control, and get out of God's way. Let's swim alongside these young radicals, giving them guidance and love, as *Rivers of Glory* burst down from Heaven, pouring out to a fatherless generation.

One

Rivers to a Generation
God Has Heard Your Cry of Pain

Lightning flashes in the distance. Thunder rumbles. The breeze picks up, cooling the old man's tears and splashing ocean spray in his face.

For days this elderly apostle, banished to an island for preaching the Gospel, has looked up beyond the veil into Heaven. Before his eyes, John has seen Jesus, looking like a slain Lamb, wounds still engraved in His human flesh (see Revelation 5:6). The glory of the Lamb has washed over the old apostle with a light more brilliant than a million suns.[1]

Now the sound of the storm increases. The wind roars. The smell of rain fills the air. John lifts his eyes to observe the coming cloudburst. What he sees takes his breath away. It's not a storm at all....It's a river.

John's heart races as he watches streams of living water tumble down to earth. Everything the river touches comes alive. Waters gleam. Fish leap. Trees blossom. Fruit grows and multiplies. Leaves heal, and dead things burst into life.

We stand today on earth, looking through John's eyes at this river. But this is not some far-off, nebulous, mystical river. It is real. It's a river of revival. Resurrection glory fills the streams, and everything the river touches comes alive.

This is the river David saw, *"whose streams make glad the City of God"* (Psalm 46:4). It's the river Ezekiel saw, pouring from the Temple (see Ezekiel 47). This is the river once closed up in the Garden of Eden (see Genesis 2:10).

You see, ever since the closing of Eden, the river of life was bottled up in the heart of the Lamb. God sent Him down to earth where the Bottle was broken to spill out its rich contents. Now a river tumbles down to a whole generation. It's a river of life pouring down to wounded, abandoned, thirsty hearts.

As you read through these pages and look at the river through John's eyes, I pray these healing streams will flood down on you. For God has chosen you for this river. He has seen the ache in the soul of a fatherless generation. He has heard your cry.

The Cry

What is this anguished cry? It's a voiceless, soundless scream. A moan of hopelessness. It's a cry of unparalleled pain, wailing from the soul of a crushed generation. The cry is, *"Daddy, where are you? Why have you forsaken me?"*

But the cry goes deeper still. Boiling within the wound, is a profound sense of rage. Abandoned by earthly fathers, sometimes mothers as well, many in your generation feel abandoned by your heavenly Father. Even as His own Son cried when He was abandoned on the cross, the cry screams up into the face of God: *"My God, why have even You forsaken me?"*

Never in history have we seen such a broken, suicidal, hopeless generation.[2] This true story, told to Dave Roever by a distraught father, shows the pain:

A father had drifted off to sleep one night when he heard his son Jeffrey slam his bedroom door. At the moment, the sound of his son opening the breach on his shotgun and sliding a shell into the chamber, didn't register. But the sound of the breach closing sent the father into a panic.

He could feel the blood rushing to his feet, leaving his brain empty. Before the full realization dawned on him, he heard the explosion. The sound still haunts him, causing him to awaken at night in a cold sweat.

"My four-year-old got there first," he told Roever. "He is still in counseling. I arrived seconds later. Jeffrey's heart was blown out and blood was everywhere. I grabbed him as he was falling over, dying." Then Jeffrey looked up with hopeless eyes and said, "I'm so sorry. I'm so sorry."

As this anguished dad held his dying son, he clung to him and cried, "Jeffrey, I love you! I love you!" Then he said, "My God, Dave, it was the first time in his life I ever told him I loved him!"

Minutes passed before this broken man could continue telling Roever his story. "Then he slumped in my arms and died. I didn't have time to get involved in the things Jeffrey wanted to do," he sighed. "I was too busy making money. But I would give it all if I could just hold him in my arms for even one minute."

The memory of holding his dead son in his arms still haunts him. "His blood was all over my hands," he said. "I looked at them and cried, 'Oh, Jesus, his blood is on my hands!'[3]

In one sense, our whole baby boomer generation could say the same thing. We have blood on our hands. So many broken homes, scattered families, wounded spirits, abused children, aborted babies, lonely teenagers — and we wonder why the suicide rate has tripled since 1950 for those between the ages of eighteen and twenty-four.[4]

Yes, there is a cry of pain rising up from the soul of a young generation. It's the cry of broken young men and women. Because so many dads were gone from home, driven by work or driven out by alcohol or other dependencies, many feel like you never really had a dad. Once the divorce shattered and scattered your family, you were even more alone.[5]

To make matters worse, as moms struggled to put food on the table, we left you in day care or home alone as the first "latchkey" kids in history. We didn't understand how abandoned and alone this made you feel. We left you with an open wound in your heart. The wound still bleeds, for bleeding flesh will heal with time but bleeding hearts do not.

Even if your family didn't divide, your friends' families did, so you all bear the scars. That's why your generation has been called "a fatherless generation."

Where Were You, Jesus?

One night a youth group from North Carolina visited our camp. Some of our revival students presented a drama which touched a raw nerve:

"Where were You, Jesus, when my parents divorced and I cried alone at night?" shouted Daniel. Angela charged up, pushing Jesus and crying, "Where were You when my birth mother didn't want me and then I was molested as a child?"

"Yeah, Jesus, where were You when my dad ran off with another woman and took another boy for his son?" blurted Corey, slapping Jesus in the face. Cathy screamed, "Where were You when I was drunk every night? Didn't You care?"

These words, flung like fists in God's face, gave voice to the pain in the soul of your whole generation. Maybe you, too, have lifted a fist and cried out, "Why, God? Why would You let me suffer like this? Where were You when I was hurting? Don't You even care?"

Now Ryan, playing the role of Jesus, threw himself to his knees and cried out to God for those who blamed him: "Father, forgive them! They don't know what they're saying. They're so hurt, but, O Father, why can't they know how much I love them?"

These words, pouring from Ryan's heart, were not just playacting. His own life had been ripped apart by his parents' divorce. Ryan had left home, living on the streets, stealing to stay alive, taking every drug he could find, desperately trying to dull the pain.

One night, while high on drugs, he knew he was dying. He cried out to God to save him, and he gave his whole life to Jesus Christ. He came here to our Bible school. When I saw his passion, I invited him to come on staff at our camp.

Now, playing the role of Jesus, Ryan knew what Jesus had done for him. His heart had been pierced by the Lamb. Often I would hear him praying, "Jesus, You drank the cup for me! For the rest of my life I will preach only Jesus Christ and Him crucified! Pierce my heart every day with Your piercings. May I always feel Your wound in my heart!"

As Ryan prayed in the garden, suddenly lightning struck the ground a few acres away, adding intensity to the drama. "Father, if it's possible, let this cup pass from Me!" Ryan continued. The heavens rumbled with thunder, and a group of soldiers flung themselves on Jesus, screaming, kicking, beating, and nailing Him to a cross. Blood spilled down His face and chest and arms and hands.

Ryan cried Jesus' last words, then hung His head and died. Moments passed. Then Ryan stepped down from the cross and walked around to the teenagers, who were sitting in stunned silence. He held out a bloody hand in front of their eyes. Walking up to one young man, he cried "Kyle, this blood is for you!"

Kyle looked away in shame. Having grown up in the church, he had been told about Jesus' blood many times, but it never meant anything. He was back on drugs now, popping pills on the bus all the way down to camp. "Kyle, your blood is on My hands!"

Kyle broke. The reality of the blood of Jesus struck his heart. Suddenly, a revelation of the love of a bleeding Savior pierced him. It was just as Charles Spurgeon said, "When we look upon the Pierced One, the piercing of our own heart begins." Kyle wept. He shook. He lay down, crying out to God.

By the end of the week he was transformed. His mom told me, "He is completely different. I've prayed so long for him, but now there's a fire inside him."

Do you see what touched him? Just one drop, one look at the blood of Jesus—though only in a drama— broke a young man open and changed him forever. For nothing so melts the heart as a long, steady look at God's Lamb.

I wish I could describe what happened next, for once the heart opens, the river of God's presence can flow in. Revival students, who had come out to the camp to pray for this youth group, formed two lines for prayer. Now, each teenager walked slowly through the tunnel of prayer as students touched them lightly and cried: *"More, Lord!"* *"Fill her with Your fire!"* *"Consume him with Your love!"* *"Let Your glory fill her heart!"* *"Holy Spirit, come! Let Your river flow!"*

The teenagers stumbled through the prayer tunnel. Some had to be carried because the Spirit of God had come down so powerfully they couldn't walk. Most of them ended up on their faces, crying and laughing and shaking in the presence of God. By the end of the week they testified of giving up drugs, immoral sex, drinking, and apathy. Most of all, passion for Jesus burned in their young hearts.

As I listened to their stories, I stood back and wept, knowing God was healing something deep in the soul of a fatherless generation. Now, after years of ministry here at our revival camp as well as five years of teaching at the ministry school, I've seen the Holy Spirit reach in with the divine scalpel of the cross. With careful precision He has lifted the scabs, cleansed out the poison, then filled the holes in the soul with rushing rivers of life.

A Real Encounter

One day I sat listening as Mary Clay, part of our revival team, told her story in two secular public schools in England, her homeland. With heartfelt sincerity, she told how she had always lived for the weekends so she could go clubbing. A snicker rippled through the audience as the students looked knowingly at one another. Though her parents were pastors of an evangelical church, she only lived to party wildly. Yet deep inside, she felt trapped. She hated her life. Once she hurled a mirror at the door, breaking it into pieces. Then she cut her arms with the broken glass.

"Though I had no fear or reverence for God, deep inside I was crying out to Him for help," she told the students. One night she took an overdose of ecstasy and felt herself dying, sinking into hell. Shortly afterward she was on her way to a three-month holiday in America, Pensacola being her first place to visit. She had only been here a few days before the Holy Spirit broke her with conviction. She gave her life to the Lord, but then He started unfolding to her the depths of the cross.

The students sat transfixed, for she was telling their story. After explaining the power of the cross, she cried, her voice breaking, "That's why I'm so free today — because Jesus is *so real!*"

But isn't this what your generation is looking for? You are searching for something *real*. You've seen the manipulation and materialism of much of Western Christianity. You've seen the hype on television and in some meetings. You've breathed the stale air of religion and it has left you dry.

One night, at the Brownsville Revival, Mary and I prayed in the parking lot for a group visiting from England. Mary laid hands on a broken, hungry young girl. Within moments, the girl was on the pavement, stiff as a board, unable to move under the power of God. We later learned she had called her mom in England that day, saying, "Mum, I just don't think any of this revival stuff is real." That night she called home, crying, "Mum, it's real! It's really *real!*"

Yes, your generation is looking for something authentic to believe. You've been so disillusioned by the broken promises of our generation that it's hard to trust anymore. But when you have a real encounter with the living God, you grab hold like a thirsty person grasping for a bottle of water in the midst of a desert. One sip and the passion within you begins to stir. Your numb heart begins to beat again. As a pastor's son told me, "It was like electrodes had been applied to my dead heart!"

Is your heart a little numb? Do you need a fresh drink from the river of God? God wants to fill you, but He only looks for one essential quality — thirst.

Thirsty for the River

Jesus said, *"If anyone is THIRSTY, let him come to me and drink...and out of his innermost being will flow rivers"* (John 7:37-38). Desperate thirst is the one requirement, for rivers always flow into the parched and thirsty places of the earth. Are you a little dry? Are you longing after God with a burning thirst?

Tommy Tenney says, "The volume of your emptiness determines the amount of your filling."[6] Are you so thirsty for more that you're willing to run after God with all your heart? Like the woman with the issue of blood, are you willing to press through and stretch out desperately for the hem of His robe?

Are you like Moses, pleading with God for more till your face gleams so brightly with the glory of God, you almost need a veil to cover the shining? Are you like the psalmist, panting after God as the deer pants for the waterbrooks? Are you like the Syrophoenician woman, begging the Lord to feed even the dogs under the table? Are you like the widow, pleading with the unjust judge for bread? Are you truly hungry for more of God? Will you be passionate for His presence?

It's like the true story of Glenn, the boy who came early to light the potbellied coal stove for his schoolhouse. One morning the teacher arrived to find the school engulfed in flames. Glenn was dragged out, but the lower half of his body was terribly burned. Doctors said he would never walk again.

Glenn, however, was determined to walk. Every day he wheeled his chair out to the picket fence in his yard, grabbed the fence, pulled himself from the chair, and dragged his legs around the yard. Finally he was able to stand, then to walk, though haltingly. He began to limp to school, then to walk, then to run. In college he tried out for the track team. Years later, at Madison Square Garden, a crowd leapt to their feet as Glenn Cunningham — the boy with the burned and crippled legs — ran the world's fastest mile.[7]

This is the passionate determination God is looking for in you. It's the thirst He loves to fill. He says, *"You will seek me and find me when you seek me with all your heart"* (Jeremiah 29:13). And the wonder is — the more you drink, the thirstier you will become.

The New Wineskin

You see, God is doing something new on this earth. Rivers of new wine are flooding down into a new wineskin.

Your whole generation is the wineskin, for He has especially targeted you who are young to receive this bubbling essence. Those of us who are older can receive it, too, but we must come with humility and thirst, willing to strip off all dignity and become like little children.

Take one sip, and you'll see—this wine is better than any the world can offer. It refreshes the soul, it heals the wounded heart, and the only hangover is more joy, more love, and more passion for Jesus.

God has saved this best wine for last because you have been chosen for this revival. And though your heart has been carved with pain, it has been broken open to receive this refreshing new wine. So open wide and begin to drink. Let streams of life and power and anointing and healing and joy and revival and, most of all, the Father's love flow down to you.

Now, as you read on through these pages, come let the healing waters wash over your own wounds, for before you can feel, you must heal. Your whole generation is a riverbed for His glory, but before you can receive more of His glory, you must let Him remove the stones from the riverbed of your own soul.

The healing comes as you lay your heart in the river of life and look up at the Wounded Lamb. Then slowly you'll find the scabs on your wounds softening and the numbness subsiding. Your heart will begin to feel again as you open wide to receive *Rivers of Glory* to a wounded generation.

Endnotes

1. See my book *The Glory of the Lamb* (Hagerstown, MD: McDougal Publishing, 2004). This book tells about the glory of Christ, through John's eyes, before creation, all through the Old Testament, throughout the days of His flesh on earth, during His crucifixion, resurrection, ascension, and glorification in Heaven. Order from your local bookstore.

2. Approximately twelve people between the ages of 15 and 24 die every day of suicide in America. Suicide rates for those between the ages of 10 and 14 have increased 99% between 1980 and 1997, with a slight decline in the last two years (Washington, DC: The American Association of Suicidology, www.suicidology.org).

3. Dave Roever with Karen Crews Crump, *Nobody's Ever Cried for Me* (Fort Worth, TX: Roever Communications, 2002), pp. 70-75. If you want to see someone who is making a difference with the kids of this nation, look at Dave Roever. Read his book and your heart will weep.

4. George Barna, *Generation Next: What You Need to Know About Today's Youth* (Ventura, CA: Regal Books, 1995), p. 24.
Stephen Arterburn and Jim Burns point out that 73% of all young people today have thought about suicide (Stephen Arterburn and Jim Burns, *When Love Is Not Enough* [Colorado Springs, CO: Focus on the Family Publishing, 1992], p. 10).

5. Arterburn and Burns explain that among the 27% of young people who have actually attempted suicide, they have experienced parental loss before the age of twelve; the parents may be talking about divorce or separation; a history of depression exists within the family; a parent was chronically ill during the young person's adolescence; the child has been sexually or physically abused (Arterburn and Burns, *When Love Is Not Enough*, p. 10).

6. Tommy Tenney, *The God Chasers* (Shippensburg, PA: Destiny Image, 1998) p. 97.

7. Jack Canfield and Mark Victor Hansen, "The Power of Determination," *Chicken Soup for the Soul* (Deerfield Beach, FL: Health Communications, 1993), pp. 256-260.

Two

Drench Your Pain in the River

Healing Your Wounds in His Wounds

John feels the moisture of the waters filling the atmosphere. He watches in awe as currents roar down from Heaven. His own heart surges with life. Though he is over ninety years old, fresh power fills every cell of his body.

He lifts his eyes higher and tries to focus on the headwaters of this river. He catches his breath as he begins to see the waters rushing down from the throne. Then he cries, "Oh, Jesus! The river flows down from *You!* You — the Lamb of God — are the fountainhead of this glorious river!"

John's thoughts slip back again to the day he first saw God's Son become the Lamb, for this was the first release of the river.

Once again, let's follow John back to that turning point of all human history. Let's behold the Lamb of God. See the One who came down from Eternity so He could know the feeling of a tear welling in His eye and sliding down the skin of His cheek. Look at the One who feels your pain, who longs to wipe away each tear and flood you with His river.

Behold the Lamb

Come climb the grassy slope and stand on the crest of the hill. Hear the cries. Feel the emotion crackle through the air. Drink in the passion. Breathe in the wonder.

Let your eyes fill with the vision of Jesus. See the one Man on earth who knows what real pain is like. Gaze into His face. See dark currents etching down His brow, spilling from the puncture wounds gourged in His brow. Watch red streams, running into His ears and nose. Gaze into His eyes, swollen from blows to His face, bloodshot from sleeplessness.

Please don't look away. Don't hide your eyes from the grinding pain of Calvary. Let the piercings of the Pierced One soften the walls protecting your heart. It may hurt, but it will heal the wounds in your soul.

One reason the Church seems shallow is because we've failed to behold the Lamb until our hearts are broken. Most of us have cried more tears over the death of a dog than over the death of our Lord.

But your generation is different. The wound in your heart aches to be filled with something real. You long for an encounter with God that will wipe away the pain and flood you with true joy.

So focus on Jesus. See His flesh shredded by the Roman scourge. As the *flagellum* lashed across the naked back of Jesus, first it cut through tender skin, laying it raw and open. The cruel scourge rutted deeper into the tissue, hacking into muscles, ripping into gristle and bone.

Blow after blow continued, severing arteries and nerves and even organs. Blood bathed His whole body. The beating Jesus endured did not simply plow open His back like the blades of a tractor plowing a field. But leather strands, studded with sharp metal prongs, slashed down across His arms and shoulders and buttocks and legs, probably even His face.

As the whip curled around His chest, it tore out great chunks of flesh, leaving Him mutilated, *"unrecognizable as a man"* (Isaiah 52:14). Men had been known to have eyes torn from their sockets, organs and entrails ripped from their bodies. That's why Jewish law permitted no more than thirty-nine lashes.

Please don't think that, because He was God enrobed in human skin, He didn't feel pain. Remember, He chose to place Himself in the same human flesh you have. He could feel every hack and rip of the scourge, every tearing of tissue and nerves, every drop of seeping blood.

But why? Why must He endure such intense suffering, flayed like a sacrificial lamb?

Why Did He Do It?

There is one supreme reason.....*You.*

He wanted to feel the depth of your pain and hurt. He

heard you secretly crying alone in the night, even as He wept alone in the garden. He saw the tears soaking your pillow in private. He felt you choking back the feelings, bottling them inside until the pressure caused a constant ache in your heart.

He saw your loneliness, even in the midst of a crowd. He felt the pain of hopelessness, which would settle over your generation like a suffocating blanket. He saw the deep wells of grief buried in your soul. He saw how our generation would fail you, leaving you with a wound that would never cease throbbing.

He watched your anguish when your parents split apart and it felt like a meat cleaver had chopped right through the center of your heart, never to mend again. He saw how the core of your being seemed severed in two separate pieces, but Jesus felt it with you.

Have you been abused? When you were too young and helpless to defend yourself, were you violated and used for another's sick pleasure? Have you ever been beaten or molested? Has your heart been hacked up by words of rejection? Did you feel like something inside had been cut into pieces? If so, then please know this—Jesus felt it with you.

He too knew the shame of nakedness and humiliation. He too experienced violence and torture. He too knew the disgrace and indignity of being wrongly violated, and of being rejected by those He loved. It helps so much to know—Jesus understands.

It's like the nineteen-year-old whose hand was caught in machinery at work and ripped from his arm. That night in the hospital, he was deeply depressed and in pain. When his pastor came to visit, he refused to see him. The pastor insisted and waited patiently while the boy kept his face to the wall.

Finally, in disgust, the boy turned over. What he saw drew a sudden gasp of shock. He had never known that his pastor had only one arm. The man had removed his prosthesis and was standing there with one sleeve empty. The boy shot upright as tears started down his cheeks. The pastor sat down beside him and held out his good arm. The boy fell against his chest, weeping. "Son," he said quietly, "I really understand."

So does Jesus. No matter what you've been through, He has been there already.

So come, through John's eyes, to look up again at Jesus. Gaze at the spikes driven through His healing hands. Soldiers had stretched His arms out across the wood. Tying ropes to His arms to keep His hands from tearing loose, they had poised a spike in the palm of each hand.[1] A soldier had lifted the hammer and slammed it down on the head of the spike.

As cold iron drilled through warm flesh, pain shivered through every nerve and cell of Jesus' body. A nerve in His palm snapped, causing His fingers to draw up in a claw as though He was grasping for His Father. His hands purpled and numbed.

Jesus groaned in pain, then softly spoke. Two criminals screamed curses as they were nailed, but what did Jesus do? He prayed. *"Father, forgive them, for they don't know what they're doing."* The reason they don't know what they're doing is because they don't know they are nailing God to a cross.[2]

Listen carefully as the same words spill over and over from His lips: *"Father, forgive them...."*[3] Can you believe it? Even as a flower is crushed to give off its fragrance, Jesus is crushed to release the fragrance of forgiveness to His enemies. Even as the grape is pressed to release its liquid, Jesus is pressed to release the liquid fruit of love.

Now He calls you to forgive those who've crushed you. But how do you forgive when the wound is so deep? How do you let go when the other person isn't even sorry? Sometimes it's so hard to forgive.

Mother and Father Wounds

One night at our camp, we ministered to a group of Teen Challenge boys. Some of them seemed a little resistant to revival, but I really felt it was due to hardness of heart, which usually comes from pain.

That night after the service, I stood before them and knelt down. I looked them in the eyes and said, "I want to stand in for your moms right now and say something you need to hear. I want to tell you how sorry I am that I couldn't stay married to your dad. I am so sorry for the pain and shame this caused you as you tried to grow up without a father."

As I spoke from my heart, something started happening in the room. Each young man grew quiet, almost stunned by my words. I could see their faces flush and tears well up in their eyes.

"I tried so hard to provide for you," I cried. "But we didn't have much money and I know you didn't have nice clothes like the other kids. I'm so sorry for the shame of poverty you experienced." I continued, "My heart aches for the way you were left alone so much while I worked. I know you felt lonely and rejected. No boy should have to suffer such loneliness. It was so wrong...."

You see, when pain drives into a tender young heart, scabs form over the hole, then scars. The poison of bitterness festers in the wound, causing hot tempers, unexplained anxiety, depression, and a deep ache inside. The heart becomes calloused and hard. Jesus wants to carefully lift the scab, pour in healing oil, wash out all the poison, soothe away the pain, and fill the hole with a river of joy.

I knew, however, that the father wounds dug even deeper in the hearts of these young men. Gordon Dalbey, in *Father and Son*, writes, "I have discovered that inside every business suit, every pair of faded overalls...lies the wounded heart of a boy longing for his daddy." Says Dalbey, "The vast majority of men in our society today are imprisoned and crippled by a voice that tells us we do not measure up as men."[4] Stephen Strang says, "When it comes to a father's love, silence is crippling, not golden."[5]

So when I finished, Ron, a man whose own father had rejected him, stood and said, "I know how you guys feel because I was abandoned by my dad. With gentle humility, he said, "Now I'd like to stand in for your dad and repent to you for the abandonment."

"I am so sorry for the way I abused your mom because of my drinking and fooling around with women." By now, the boys were openly weeping. Two of them were sobbing uncontrollably. They later told how they had seen their own fathers beat their moms when they were too young to protect them. The anger and guilt they had stuffed down inside had erupted in rage, alcoholism, drug addictions, and even crime.

Ron continued to repent for the rejection and abandonment, explaining that the main reason their dads rejected them was because of their own father wounds. For the next four hours we listened to their stories and led them in prayers of repentance for bitterness and of forgiveness of parents. We even had a foot washing to symbolize washing away the old and stepping into the new.

The next day, our revival students formed two lines for a river tunnel. Again the power of the Lord came down. I watched these young men walk through a tunnel of anointing, as students prayed with all their hearts. The Holy Spirit fell upon these Teen Challenge boys, whose hearts were now cleansed from bitterness, and they came undone. Every one of them was touched by God's power. Strong young men shook, they fell to the grass, they cried like babies in the presence of Jesus.

The Holy Spirit drenched each one of them with the waters of refreshing. But it was because they had first let Him wash away their bitterness. Forgiveness had cleansed their wounds and prepared them for the river. Their leader told me later, "In all my years of working with Teen Challenge, I have never seen our boys so filled with passion for Jesus Christ!"

I Repent to You

Now let me talk to you personally. I want to stand in for your parents and repent. I want to take your hand, look into your eyes, and ask your forgiveness for what my generation did to you. As I talk to you, picture the face of the one who has hurt you.

I am terribly, terribly sorry for all that you have been through. My heart aches for the hurt you have endured. I grieve for the words of criticism and ridicule your young ears may have heard. It was so wrong.

I am so sorry for the times I got angry and called you bad names. That was wrong. I'm sorry for the times you spent alone. I hurt for the tears you cried when no one was around.

Your mom or dad may even have died, making you feel so lonely. Or you may have been adopted, making you wonder if you're really wanted.

Deep inside you feel angry and all alone. I wish I could let you cry on my shoulder like you would to a mom. If you were here, I would say to you, "Let it all out. Don't hold anything back. Don't be afraid to cry, for the pockets of hidden grief need to come out."

I want to tell you how hurt I am for you guys who grew up without a dad. This probably made you feel unsure of your manhood. Even if he was there, he was probably emotionally absent. You needed a dad to relate to as a man. This wounded your own identity.

If you're a young lady who always longed for the love of a man, I wish I could be there to minister God's love to you. You may have given up your virginity, hoping to gain the love you seek, only to find that your boyfriend abandoned you, too. There's really only One who'll never use you or leave you.

Only Jesus.

Now, with God's burden for you burning in my heart, I want to stand as a parent and say to you, *I'm sorry. We were wrong.* The divorce tore your world apart. The loneliness hurt to the core of your being. The abandonment robbed your identity. It was wrong, but I am asking—will you please forgive me? Will you forgive us?

Powerless to Forgive

I realize what a difficult request that is, but if you will forgive, it will release the infection within you. There's probably some buried grief that needs to be removed, but we'll minister to your grief in the next chapter.

For now, we need to get the bitterness out. There's only one way. It's God's time-honored way of confession, repentance, and cleansing with His blood.

So look up again at Jesus. See the One who was willing to forgive His enemies. See blood spilling from every wound. Watch the tears dripping from His eyes, soaking into patches of His beard. If you will kneel down before Him, asking the Holy Spirit to help you, He will wash the poison out of your wounds.

Keep your focus on Him and lay your heart bare. Tell Him why you are angry. Tell Him who you are angry with. Be gut-level honest with Him. Name your sin as *sin*. Call it resentment. Bitterness. Hatred. Murder. Fear. Whatever describes the sin, name it and lay it before Him. For the blood of Jesus never cleanses excuses; it only cleanses sin.

Now look into His loving eyes and tell Him you are sorry. Mean it with all your heart. Ask for a gift of repentance, godly sorrow for the sin. I know the other person was terribly wrong. That's not the point. You need to be free of the poison of bitterness, so tell Jesus how truly sorry you are.

See Him, bleeding from every gash in His body. Talk to Him. He understands. If you will repent, you can be sure of this—His blood will wash you perfectly clean. Let that blood come on you. His blood carries the DNA of God. It is powerful to take away sin. It's just like the Bible says, *"The blood of Jesus, his Son, purifies us from all sin"* (1 John 1:7).

Put yourself beneath those drops of blood falling from His wounds. Picture a crimson waterfall flooding down over you. Let every sin be drowned in the Red Sea of your Savior's blood.

If you will believe you are cleansed, you are. I know it sounds too simple, but Christianity is simple. We have made it complicated.

Now ask the Holy Spirit to give you the grace to forgive. Say, "I am powerless to forgive, so please help me, Holy Spirit." Ask Him to forgive through you.

Remember this: The reason this one has rejected you is because of his or her own wounds, probably a father wound. See the same blood that cleansed you, flooding over this one. Now bless this person, as Jesus said, *"Bless those who curse you, pray for those who mistreat you"* (Luke 6:28).

But we're not done. Here comes the hard part. You need to forgive yourself. You see, Jesus has forgiven you, but if you don't forgive yourself, it's like saying, "Your sacrifice was not enough! Your blood was shed in vain for me!" It's like nailing Him again to the cross.

So go look in your own eyes in a mirror. Say to yourself, "I forgive you, (*your name*)." Say it again until you mean it. Forgive yourself until you can feel the forgiveness flowing in and you are completely free.

Now lay your own hand over Your heart. Whisper, "Father, fill me with your love." Let His love flow in. Receive. Let Him wash your wounds and fill the void with the love of a real Dad.

After all, isn't that what you've always wanted? A relationship with a faithful Father. Let Him be to you the Dad you may never have had. He's a Father to a fatherless generation, *drenching your pain in the river* that flows from the Lamb of God.

Endnotes

1. I disagree with those who insist the spikes were driven through Jesus' wrists. The soldiers tied ropes to Jesus' arms which kept His hands from tearing loose. The Bible doesn't say it was His wrists, but His hands: Zechariah 13:6, margin; Isaiah 49:16; Luke 24:39; John 20:20, 25, 27. That's one reason blessings still fall from His hands in Heaven, for the hands that bled now bless.

2. Scriptures proving that Jesus is God are the following: John 1:1, 14; John 8:19; John 14:9, 11; Philippians 2:6. If this is difficult to understand, remember that in the Godhead there is God the Father, God the Son, and God the Holy Spirit. They are three separate beings, yet one in the Godhead. Jesus is God the Son in human flesh.

3. The Greek tense indicates that He said, *"Father, forgive them...."* over and over.

4. Gordon Dalbey, *Father and Son: The Wound, the Healing, the Call to Manhood* (Nashville: Thomas Nelson Publishers, 1992), pp. 5, 8.

5. "I have my own father-wound," writes Stephen Strang in *Old Man, New Man*, "and I've never known a man who didn't have one" (Stephen Strang, *Old Man, New Man* [Lake Mary, FL: Creation House, 2000], pp. 16-17).

Three

Soak Your Grief in the River
Jesus Cried the Cry of Your Generation

John's heart trembles now as he thinks of this mountain peak of all time when the Lamb released His pent-up flood. He squints the eyes of his spirit and looks more intently at the river, flowing down *"from the throne of God and of the Lamb"* (Revelation 22:1).

Suddenly, he sees it. There it is…the wound in His side. "Oh, Lord Jesus!" he cries. "The river flows down from the wound in Your side!"

John knows. He was there. He saw the soldier drive the spear into Jesus. It pierced all the way up to the lining of His heart, where blood and water poured out (see John 19:34).

John's thoughts slip back now to the moment when Jesus cried the saddest words ever heard upon this earth. This is the moment in time when God Himself cried your cry.

The Saddest Cry on Earth
In the distance a dark cloud creeps toward Calvary. The

sun vanishes. The sky turns black. An eerie darkness covers the land.

Now a hush falls over the crowd at the foot of the cross. Even Mary, weeping softly in John's arms, lifts her head, startled by the sudden darkness. At His birth it was bright at midnight; now at His death, it is midday and the sky is black as night.

Suddenly, a look of terror fills Jesus' eyes. His forehead creases. He shuts His eyes tightly. He writhes in agony on the cross. Raw wounds on His back scrape against the wood, but He seems oblivious of the physical pain.

Something hideous has fallen upon Him. Though He hangs in absolute weakness, blood streaming from every rip in His flesh, He is bearing the sins of the world in Himself. The Bible says that He became sin (see 2 Corinthians 5:21) as He sagged there from two stakes of wood.

God has taken the sins of all humanity and rolled them down on His innocent Son. He is, as John the Baptist said, *"the Lamb of God who takes away the sin of the world."* Jesus is taking away sin by taking it into Himself. That's why He thrashes in terror.

Think what this means to you. He is not simply carrying all humanity's sin, but all your sins are falling down and pressing into Jesus. All your pride and doubt, your drug addictions, your sexual impurity, your hatred and rage are pouring down on Him.

Though your transgressions crush Him, He must take

your sin so you can have His presence. He loves you so much He cannot bear to live without you.

But suddenly, Jesus stops thrashing under the weight of sin. His body stiffens. He becomes rigid. His face pales. His eyes fly open wide.

The look in His eyes is too deep to comprehend. It is a look of terror. Something even more gruesome than sin has fallen upon the Savior, causing Him to scream the cry of your generation.

Watch now as He presses down hard on the nail in His feet, lifting His lungs for air. This sudden push tugs open the wound in His feet. Blood spurts afresh, spilling down His feet and toes, dripping down and puddling on the ground.

Look back up at His face. See Jesus' swollen eyes, as He now forces them open and rolls His gaze upward. Study His eyes. They are filled with untold horror. They show the utter grief and fear of abandonment.

Yes, in the midst of unthinkable pain from throbbing wounds and dripping blood, while struggling under this terrible weight, Jesus cries alone.

Now He throws back His head. Jesus' mouth flies open wide, as though He's about to speak. For the last three hours He hasn't said a word. In the first three hours He spoke three times, once to forgive His murderers, next to save a thief, and third to release His mother to John's protective care.

For these last three hours, however, He's been unable to

speak. The pain is too deep for words. The agony chokes away His breath.

But now, with His mouth open, His eyes turned upward toward Heaven, and His lungs full, Jesus is about to speak. Inch in a little closer and listen....

For a moment time stands still. The frenzied crowd hushes. Priests and Romans stand petrified. Tension charges the atmosphere. Emotion thunders in every breast.

Suddenly, Jesus explodes with a roaring shriek, *"Eli, Eli, lama sabachthani?"* The words, which are a mixture of Aramaic and Hebrew, mean, *"My God, My God, why have You forsaken Me?"* (Matthew 27:46, NKJ).

This is what Bible scholars call "the cry of dereliction." It gives a window into His suffering, for God has forsaken God. Jesus has cried this cry alone. It's the saddest cry ever heard on earth, but it answers the cry of your heart.

Think about those times when you were all by yourself. Those moments when you cried alone in the darkness. You thought He didn't hear your muffled cry, but He did. He looked down from Eternity and listened to the silent screams of fear when you were abused or abandoned. He saw the bitterness and fury when you were rejected and left alone. His heart ached when He felt the grief quietly pulsing behind the walls of your soul.

He heard the moan of anguish issuing up from the soul of a fatherless generation. He heard your cry, "Daddy, where are you?" He listened to the sob, "My God, why have *even You* abandoned me?" You thought the cry was voiceless, but He saw you soak your pillow with tears and cry, "Why, God? Why don't You even care? Why have You forsaken me?"

Do you see now why Jesus cried that anguished heart cry, the saddest cry ever heard upon this earth?

There are many reasons, but this one must not be overlooked — He cried your cry so you would never have to cry it again. He wept your tears and sobbed the pain of your soul so He could run to the sound of your cry:

> *For because He Himself [in His humanity] has suffered .... He is able* [immediately] *to run to THE CRY of...those who are being tempted, tested and tried* [and who therefore are being exposed to suffering].
> Hebrews 2:18, AMP

So I urge you, the next time trouble comes, don't lift your fist to rail at God. Lift your eyes to Calvary, and let Jesus heal your grief. In fact, before you read on, if you feel tears welling up inside, stop and tell the Lord just how you feel.

Lay your hand on your heart and whisper, "Holy Spirit, please come and soften the walls protecting my heart. Help me get in touch with buried grief, so I can get out all the pain."

Getting Grief Out

When I pray for people at church or at camp, I sometimes see one whose heart seems hurt or very hard. Often

I'll place the other person's hand over his or her heart and lay my hand on top. Then I simply pray for the Holy Spirit to pour in His love. Almost every time, I begin to feel hot tears dripping on my hand. "Let all the grief out," I'll say, holding the person as he or she sobs on my shoulder.

When I feel the tears subside, I'll lay my hand softly on the person's head and ask the Holy Spirit to come. Usually, the Holy Spirit will fill the person so full he or she can't stand up and will fall to the floor, resting in His presence or laughing with joy.

You see, there's great power in getting the grief out. Grief is like the lock on a door. Until the dead bolt unlocks, it's hard to pry open the door to forgiveness. Sometimes, before the bitterness and rage can be removed, the key on the dead bolt needs to be turned.

Repressed grief creates the soil in which bitterness, resentment, hatred, anger, and rage grow like ugly weeds. Before the weeds of hatred can be pulled, the hard ground of grief must be softened with tears.

Psychiatrist Erick Linderman tells about a young nurse who cared for her dying father. She often choked back the tears, burying her pain as she nursed him. When he died, for the sake of her mother whose heart was weak, she refused to show her grief. Linderman said that within hours the young nurse developed ulcerative colitis from repressed grief. Eventually she died, "killed by the suppressed grief she would not allow herself to express in copious tears."[1]

Grief comes, not only over death, but also from severed

relationships, shattered promises, divided families, broken dreams. Canyons filled with grief ache beneath the surface. This is why people feel so much better after a good cry. Crying releases chemicals in the brain that build up from emotional pain.

It's like the little boy, when he heard that his neighbor's wife had died, who rushed to his house, ran inside, and hopped up on his lap. When he came home, his mother asked, "What did you say to him?" He quickly replied, "Nothing. I just helped him cry."[2]

Steve Hill said, "A tear is agony in solution."[3] Tears help cleanse the grief within. Holding back the tears is unhealthy, even for tough guys. [4] The concept that "real men don't cry" is a myth, said Hill. This notion has produced generations of "masculine mummies." Boys are taught, "Quench your emotions! Bite your quivering lip! Change the subject! Turn your head and take slow, deep breaths. Fight the feeling, and it will pass. You'll be marked for life if they see you sob."[5]

Jesus, however, was never ashamed to cry. He wept at Lazarus' death. He cried with *loud cries and tears* (Hebrews 5:7) in Gethsemane . He sobbed so hard in the garden that blood pressed out of His pores. He wailed over Jerusalem when He looked out over the city, and I believe He still sheds tears today.

Pure Joy
Believe me, I'm no stranger to pain and grief. Years ago

there was a time when I felt like my heart had been peeled raw, then kicked aside and stomped on. The pain was so deep I could hardly breathe. I cried every day and feared I couldn't stop crying. Depression swallowed me, because I held so much pain inside.

One night, in the spring of 1995, while in seminary, I walked into a revival at Harvest Rock Church in Pasadena, California. At first, the manifestations of revival offended me, but the Lord had told me He was bringing revival to America and He wanted me to "avail myself of every opportunity to drink from this river." At the end of the service, I went forward for prayer, and my life was changed forever.

A little woman laid her hand lightly on my head and prayed, "Come, Holy Spirit! More, Lord!" Suddenly, I fell forward on my knees and then to my face, weeping. I didn't even know what I was crying about. It felt like something had been closed up inside and, with this touch of the Holy Spirit, my heart opened and spilled out its contents.

From that point on, while still in seminary, I began going to revival several nights a week. I discovered that if I took specific wounds to the river of God in revival, something amazing began happening. When the presence of God came down on me during the ministry time, I laid my heart bare before Him. I told the Lord how I felt. I cried out my grief in the arms of Jesus until at last the tears all poured out.

Suddenly, it was like the dead bolt unlocked and the door of forgiveness cracked open. I confessed my sin of bitterness to the Lord, and then I told Him I was powerless to forgive. I needed His help to forgive through me. He washed me clean with His blood and removed the bitterness in my soul.

After this the miracle came. Joy flooded back into the holes in my heart. I could hardly believe it. Laughter bubbled up from deep within. As refreshing joy poured through me, I laughed and laughed. It was wondrously healing. Joyfully renewing. I know some people criticize "holy laughter," but who can criticize the fruit of a healed heart?

My heart was healed, not by medicine, not by some retreat in the mountains, not by counseling, not by people at all. I found the river of revival flowing down from the heart of the Lamb. I dipped my broken heart into the healing streams until the grief spilled out, infections of bitterness and anger floated away in the cleansing streams of the river, and God filled up all the holes with pure joy.

He did this for me, and I've seen Him do it for so many others. I know He wants to do the same for you. So come to Him now in the privacy of your place of prayer. Come once again to look up at Jesus. See the wounds in His hands and feet and side.

Now tell Him how you feel. Talk to Him about the hurt. Let grief begin to surface. When the tears come, let the dam break. Don't hold back. Weep in His arms until grief streams out through your tears. Cry until the tears completely dry.

Let Him cleanse out more poison of resentment. Release your enemies with even deeper forgiveness, for once the grief is gone, it's so much easier to forgive. It's like dipping a sponge into a pool of water. First, you squeeze the dirty sponge, wringing out all the grief and bitterness. Then you let go of the sponge, and soak up fresh, clean water into the holes.

Put on some worship music now and soak in the glory of His presence. Let the new wine of Heaven drown all your sorrows. Let pain float away like logs on a rushing stream.

Now look back up to the Lord and ask Him to give you joy where once there was pain. Remember, Jesus invited a broken, used-up, discarded woman to drink from His well of living water. He said, *"The water I give you will become a spring of water bubbling up within you"* (John 4:14).

So lay your hand on your belly, and whisper, "Come, Holy Spirit; come and give me springs of bubbling joy." Wait on Him until the joy comes. Let it come. Let streams of joy fill every crevice of your soul. Let living waters fill up every crack in your heart. Let the river come until laughter and joy bubble up within you. Give way to the joy and let it flood through you like waves of the sea.

You see, this is why He cried your cry of abandonment on the cross: So you could have peace where once you had pain; so you could have His presence where once you felt forsaken; so you could have joy where once you had grief;

so you could soak your heart forever in *Rivers of Glory* flowing down from the Lamb.

Endnotes
1. William H. Frey II and Muriel Langseth, *Crying, The Mystery of Tears* (Minneapolis: Winston Press, Inc., 1985), p. 99; cited in Stephen Hill, *Time to Weep* (Orlando: Creation House, 1997), p. 61.
2. Jack Canfield and Mark Victor Hansen, *A Third Serving of Chicken Soup for the Soul* (Deerfield, FL: Health Communications, Inc., 1996), p. 12.
3. Stephen Hill, *Time to Weep*, p. 149.
4. Hubert Humphrey said, "A man without tears is a man without a heart" (William Frey II and Muriel Langseth, *Crying, The Mystery of Tears*, p. 99; cited in Stephen Hill, *Time to Weep*, p. 61).
5. Stephen Hill, *Time to Weep*, p. 57.

Four

A River of Love

When Jesus Took Your Punishment for Sin

The river roaring down from the Lamb flows down on the old apostle. Gratitude overwhelms him, for he knows these are costly waters. They are free to all who are thirsty, but Jesus paid an immeasurable price to give us this refreshing drink.

As John thinks of this cost, the cry of Jesus still rings in his mind. Once again he is there as this cry of abandonment sounds across the hills of Jerusalem, paralyzing all of nature.

Birdsongs cease. The wind stops blowing. The sun still hides its face. The clouds hover low, trembling as though ready to weep. The crowd stands mute with shock, stunned by this guttural howl of forsakenness from the lips of the Lord.[1]

Jesus' body is extremely tense. Shallow breaths rasp in and out as He struggles to take in air. His face is white with shock. His eyes are swollen shut. Grief, from screaming up at His Father, etches His brow. He hangs His head. Tears fall across His cheeks.

How could the Son shriek such a horrific cry in the face of His beloved Father? How could He wound His Father's heart like this? The reason is fathomless—Jesus has been draining the Father's cup.

What, then, is this cup? Why did a mere glimpse of this cup cause the Lord to gush bloody sweat in the garden? Why did drinking its contents wrench such a ghastly cry from His lips on the cross?

Why did Jonathan Edwards, considered one of America's greatest revival theologians, say, "Jesus' principal errand into the world was to drink *that cup*"[2]? If drinking the Father's cup of wrath against sin was Jesus' primary purpose in coming to earth, why do we hear so little about it?

These questions will be answered if you will take a long, deep look into the contents of that cup. If you will fully let the magnitude of this cup touch you, I think something will happen inside you. You will understand, as never before, how much God loves you. His love will fill you with a purpose and passion like you've never known in all your life.

So come now and look up at Jesus as He drinks His Father's cup for you.

The Cup

As a blazing inferno mounts and swells, then sweeps through a forest, burning down everything in its path, the fire of GOD'S HOLY WRATH against sin has mounted over Jesus.

Here He hangs, the Man whose only fault was love. His face drains chalk white. His body remains stiff from the grueling weight upon Him.

Now the wave breaks. It bursts down upon Him. Wave after wave of the JUDGMENT OF GOD roars down upon the innocent Son. This is the pure and undiluted fire of God's wrath. It is not a visible fire, but a spiritual blaze, burning up all your sin in Him.[3]

Indeed, the Bible says, He was *"stricken and afflicted by God, pierced for our transgressions, crushed for our iniquities. The PUNISHMENT that brought us peace was upon him"* (Isaiah 53:4-5). Yes, Jesus is being punished for your sin.

Do you realize what this means? He took God's eternal wrath against *your* sin. He endured *your* hell — the flames of wrath which you deserve for sin. Jesus did that for *you!* For *you!*

Please pause and soak that in. Let it go in deep....

Jesus saw what would happen to you if He did not drink that cup. He saw you burning in hell if He did not bear your punishment for sin in Himself.

And so, as God's wrath boils down upon the Son, Jesus takes it in. He can barely breathe. No longer does He notice the pain from bleeding wounds. The horror of eternal wrath consumes Him.

This true story helps illustrate what Jesus did. One night in 1988, an excited youth group was traveling home from a day at *Kings Island*, an amusement park in Carrollton, Kentucky. Suddenly, over the hill came the drunk driver, careening down the wrong side of the road. The bus burst into flames on impact.

John Pearman, the associate pastor of First Assembly of God in Radcliff, Kentucky, was the driver on the bus. When flames exploded through the bus, Pearman could have jumped off and saved his own life. But hearing the screams of the kids, he loved them more than he loved his own life.

Instead of running out of the blazing inferno, he grabbed the fire extinguisher. With one hand he fought to extinguish the fires; with the other, he worked to pull the teenagers out of the bus. Finally, the black spiral of smoke overwhelmed him and he passed out. He burned to death, along with twenty-seven others, mostly kids. But forty escaped, and John Pearman died a hero's death. He did everything he could to save his kids from the flames.[4]

So did Jesus. He looked out from Eternity, before the world's creation, and He saw *you*. He saw what would happen if He didn't drink the Father's cup. He saw you burning in the fires of hell. He saw your generation screaming in infinite agony. He saw you drinking *"the wine of God's fury, which has been poured full strength into the cup of his wrath"* (Revelation 14:10).

Like that love-driven hero, John Pearman, He couldn't bear to hear you screaming in the midst of the flames. So He left His Father's throne and tore through the pages of history. Racing down to Jerusalem, He threw Himself down on a cross, where He had a head-on collision with God's judgment against sin.

But always His thoughts were fixed on drinking your cup of punishment. [5] He must lay Himself on the altar of the cross so, like John Pearman, He could retrieve you from the flames of hell. [6] And so, as billows of God's wrath rushed down upon Him, He drank the Father's cup for *you*. Did you know He loved you so much?

You see, as Jesus hung in anguish on the cross, He saw your loneliness. He saw how meaningless life would seem to you. He knew you would search for answers in all the wrong places.

He saw your disgust with lifeless religion. He knew you would love Him if you could only understand how much He loves you. If you could see what He did for you when He drank the Father's cup, you would love Him forever.

That's why I ask you to look long and deep at the cup of burning wrath He drank for you. Look until you can feel the rivers of love pouring into your heart.

Your generation says, "Don't tell me how much you love me. Show me." That's what God did. He sent His Son to a cross to show you the magnitude of His love.

This is what your generation needs to hear. You need to hear about a God who loves you so much He stood in your place and was punished for your sin. You need to hear about a God who took your hell so you could have His

Heaven. This isn't a harsh message; it's a message of unfathomable love.

Won't you bring this truth to your generation? If you will, it will transform the world. But it's not only a message of Jesus' love, but of the Father's love as well. The love of the Father will heal a wounded generation.

The Father's Heart

One day in my Systematic Theology class Greg told his story, which helped us catch a glimpse of the Father's heart as He looked down on His own Son, bleeding on a cross.

Driving back from a revival service in Ohio, Greg pulled over one night to help his pastor with a flat tire. Suddenly a drunk driver slammed into Greg's car with his family inside. He tried to help his daughter and wife, but then he heard his son, crushed beneath the seats, struggling to breathe, making low gurgling sounds. His son was covered with blood and Greg knew he was dying.

Years before he had been angry with God because his son needed healing and it didn't come. One night he asked God, "How could You abandon Your own Son?" Immediately Greg saw a vision of his own little boy, only a few months old, covered with blood and beaten beyond recognition. He began to wail and moan in the presence of God. Then he heard the Lord say, "This is how I felt."

Now, however, this was not a vision. His boy was covered with blood and was unrecognizable. In that moment a daddy knew the sheer terror of seeing his own son bleeding and dying before his very eyes. He cried out to God, "God, I give You my son. I can't save him!"

Paramedics came and rushed the boy to Children's Hospital. Greg didn't know it, but on the way his son coded and was pronounced dead. Meanwhile, Greg found the drunk driver and prayed with him. He forgave him and then spoke prophetically, "This night you will see the mercy of God."

"And that's what happened!" Greg told our class, tears washing his face. We all sat breathless, drinking in his story. "The mercy of God broke through and my little boy *revived!* Today he is perfectly normal."

With a smile shining through the tears, he said, "I learned a powerful lesson.... I learned what the Father in Heaven felt when He gave His own Son for me."[7] Greg bowed his head and cried, and we were all speechless, wiping away our tears.

Of course we can't fully know what the Father felt. He gave us the true story of Abraham to show us the agony of a father called to sacrifice his son (see Genesis 22). For He wants us to know that His heart was wounded too. He was wounded by the woundings of His Son. He was grieved by the wrath He had to pour on His Beloved. He was pierced to the core of His being with the cry of His Son, *"My God, why have You forsaken Me?"*

But He did it for *you*. Not because He's cruel, but because God is holy and sin had to be punished before you could come into His presence. He punished Jesus for your sin so you could have His Heaven. Did you know He loved you this much?

God's Answer to the Fatherless

One night we tried to demonstrate this love in a drama at our camp for another group of Teen Challenge guys. As rough soldiers crucified Jesus in the background, in the foreground a father was hitting his wife and yelling at his son, Benny. "Ever since you came along, Benny, we've had trouble," screamed the dad. "I wish you had never been born!"

Benny threw himself on the ground and screamed out, just as Jesus was crying the same words from the cross: "Daddy, why have you forsaken me?"

These words struck a tender spot in these young men from broken families, drug-abusing parents, and violence in their homes. One young man with bitterness and grief in his heart had walked in on his sister hanging dead from a noose in her room.

After the drama, we gathered them under the trees in our torch-lit prayer garden. I stood in for their moms and told them how sorry I was for all the ways their moms had neglected them. Then Tony, a fifty-year-old father figure, poured his heart out in tearful repentance for all the ways their dads had hurt them. One by one, they came forward and we washed their feet and ministered to them personally. Something deep broke loose in these young men as they wept on our shoulders and forgave their moms and dads.

One young man, Philip, told how his biological dad had left home and virtually abandoned him and his mom. But Philip had loved his dad and wanted desperately to hear from him. Then, when he was eleven years old, he received news that his dad had died. Deep in his heart was a boulder of pain and bitterness.

But now Tony stood in for his dad and, with tears dripping down his face, told him how sorry he was for leaving him, how much he really loved him, and how proud he was of him. Philip cried his heart out on Tony's shoulder and completely forgave his dad. It was like a huge rock rolled away from the tomb of his heart. What happened next flooded his tomb with God's river.

A team of revival students lined our grape arbor in the prayer garden and began soaking each other with prayer. By the time the Teen Challenge boys, whose hearts had now been cleansed of bitterness and grief, walked through the tunnel, a river of love was rushing.

I watched these strong young men stumble through the tunnel, crying like babies. Soon it looked like a war zone with bodies lying all over the camp grounds. They wept, worshiped, and trembled under the power. Brandon, their leader, told me, "I've never seen these guys touched so deeply!"

Afterwards, standing around the campfire, one young man said, "I didn't know what I was looking for. I've tried to find happiness in drugs and drinking and women, but now, at last, I've found what I'm looking for. This is the greatest thing I've ever found!" Then he covered his face and burst into tears of joy.

Philip, the man whose dad had died when he was eleven, said, "At last I've found the love of a real Dad. It's the love of my heavenly Father!"

Yes, your generation is love-starved because of all the father and mother wounds. But this is God's answer for these wounds, for He promises to be *"a father to the father-less"* (Psalm 68:5). David wrote, *"Though my father and mother forsake me, the LORD will receive me"* (Psalm 27:10).

Do you see how vital this move of God's love is for your generation? The river of God changes lives. It's like applying electrodes to the nearly dead heart of a whole generation. It brings life where once there was death.

When the deer-like animal called the hart is wounded, he longs for the water brooks so he can dip his wounded limbs into the healing streams (see Psalm 42:1, KJV). Won't you do the same? Won't you come dip once again in the river of love?

We've talked about drenching your pain and soaking your grief; we've asked the Lord to fill the holes in your heart with His joy. But let's go deeper now. Let's ask Him to fill you with the Father's love.

This story illustrates the love of a father, which God wants to give you. At the Barcelona Olympics, Derek Redmond raced around the track, neck and neck with the lead runners. Suddenly the hamstring in his leg snapped and he fell to the track, rolling in agonizing pain. People hardly noticed as he pushed himself to his feet and staggered down the track, dragging his leg.

Even as the crowd cheered for the winners, an old man quietly rose from the grandstand, pushed through the crowd, and hurried to Redmond's side. Throwing his arm around him, he shouldered him to the end of the race. Who was this old man? It was Derek Redmond's dad.

That's what your heavenly Father wants to do for you. He saw you staggering down the racetrack of life, dragging a heart filled with pain. So He left the grandstand of Heaven and raced down to your side. Now He wants to throw His arm around you and carry you down the track.

Won't you lean on Him now and let Him shoulder you to the end of the race? Draw so near you can actually feel His presence surrounding you. Get so close you can sense the currents of His river of love, spilling down from above.

You see, the love of the Father is deep, secure, pure, strong, faithful, and protective. He's a Dad who will never leave you or forsake you. He will always be there to pick you up when you fall down. He will fill you with trust and security. It's the love you've looked for all of your life.

And because you're now a son or a daughter, you can cry, *"Abba, Father"* (Romans 8:15), which is the intimate name for Father God. This cry to *Abba* is "the deepest primordial cry of the human heart," says Lou Engel.[8]

Try it now. Simply whisper, *"Abba.... Abba*, Father....*Abba*, Daddy...."

Now let that love go in deep. Let the Holy Spirit carefully remove the stitches that hold your heart together. Let Jesus Himself take a golden pitcher and pour in the healing waters of the Father's love. Let the warm, loving currents pour into your heart. Let that strong, protective, trustworthy love, which you may never have had, go in deep. Let streams of His faithfulness fill and fill and fill.

And as you drink of these costly waters, let gratitude overwhelm you. For this river is free to you but it cost Him everything.

So drink your fill from this endless supply, but never, never forget the suffering that brought these sacred streams. Because the Father poured His cup of wrath on the Son, because Jesus swallowed down every drop of that cup, now you can drink forever from these *Rivers of Glory*.

Endnotes
 1. In this cry, Jesus is quoting Scripture: *"My God, my God, why have you forsaken me? Why are you so far from saving me, so far from the words of my groaning"?* (Psalm 22:1). Knowing the Hebrew language, John would know the word *groaning* from Psalm 22:1 is *sheagah*, meaning, "rumbling, moaning, mighty roaring."
 2. Jonathan Edwards wrote the following about Christ's primary purpose in coming to earth:
    His principal errand into the world was to drink that cup, and he therefore was never unthoughtful of it, but always bore it in his mind and often spoke of it to his disciples.... So he speaks of his bloody baptism (Luke 12:50), "But I have a baptism to be baptized with; and how am I straitened till it be accomplished!" He speaks of it again to Zebedee's children (Matthew 20:22), "Are ye able to drink of the cup that I shall drink of, and to be baptized with the baptism

that I am baptized with?"…. And he was very much in speaking of it a little before his agony, in his dying counsels to his disciples in the 12th and 13th ch. of John. Thus this was not the first time that Christ had this bitter cup in his view. On the contrary, he seems always to have had it in his view. But it seems that at this time God gave him an extraordinary view of it (Jonathan Edwards, "Christ's Agony," *The Works of Jonathan Edwards*, Vol. 2 [Edinburgh: Banner of Truth Trust, 1995], p. 867).

3. Scriptures on the fire of God falling on the sacrifice: Leviticus 9:23-24; 1 Kings 18:38; 1 Chronicles 21:26; 2 Chronicles 7:1.

4. Dave Roever, *Nobody's Ever Cried for Me*, pp. 103-112; "Burying a Brother," *Daily Egyptian*, Internet: http://newshound.de.sie.edu.

5. Scriptures on the Father's cup: Psalm 75:8; Jeremiah 25:15-16; Matthew 26: 39-42; Mark 14:23-36; Luke 22:42; John 18:11; Romans 3:25-26; Romans 8:3;Revelation 14:10.

6. Jonathan Edwards said that Jesus endured "the very pains of hell." The contents of the cup were "fully equivalent to the misery of the damned, for it was the wrath of the same God" (Jonathan Edwards, "Christ's Agony," pp. 868, 871). John Stott said, "We may even say that our sins sent Christ to hell," not after the cross but "before His body died" (John R. W. Stott, *The Cross of Christ* [Downers Grove, IL: InterVarsity Press, 1986, p. 79).

7. Greg and Beth Conley are members of Brownsville Assembly of God in Pensacola. He told this story in my Systematic Theology class and again in a paper he wrote for my class.

8. Lou Engel, in a message given in May 1996 at Harvest Rock Church in Pasadena, California.

Five

Rivers From His Piercing
Wiping Every Scar and Leaving Only One

John's heart shakes and tears wet his face, for he knows — he can only drink of this river of love because Jesus drank of the cup of wrath. His thoughts slip back again to the moment when Jesus fully engulfed the Father's cup and released the pent-up floods.

Jesus drinks and drinks and drinks.... As this cup of divine wrath roars down upon Him, He opens wide to take in every drop.

Look more closely at Him now. See beyond the veil of His flesh. See beyond the seeping blood and mangled tissue. Focus on His heart. Watch it swelling and filling so full with love for you that it is almost ready to burst. As He looks out and sees you, the love in His heart rises like an ocean tide.

Now the heart of this lovely, holy, innocent One can take no more. He has drained the last bitter drop of the Father's cup, and His heart, so swollen with love and sorrow, now smashed with the wrath of God, is almost ready to break open.

Watch Jesus now as He gives His final words. He cries out with thirst, and a soldier wets His tongue with cheap wine vinegar. Then He shouts triumphantly the sixth word from the cross: *"It is finished!"* (John 19:30, NKJ). Now every demon falls crushed beneath His feet, for even as He finished the work of creation on the sixth day, He finishes the work of redemption with His sixth word.

And even as God rested on the seventh day, He enters His rest with His seventh word: *"Father, into your hands I commit my spirit"* (Luke 23:46).

Now, with this final cry, it happens... The heart of the Lamb of God bursts open. Physicians today say He died of heart rupture as indicated by blood and water pouring out separately (see John 19:34). It is just as the Scripture says, *"I am poured out like water,... My heart is like wax; it is softened [with anguish] and melted down within me"* (Psalm 22:14, AMP).

You see, nails didn't kill Him; blood loss from beatings didn't end His life; He didn't die of asphyxiation or from the soldier's spear. Jesus died of a ruptured heart from drinking His Father's cup.

Stand back now and see the Master's head, hanging across His chest. Blood-drenched hair droops across His brow. His hands dangle limply from iron spikes. Jesus' body is a bloody pulp, but the sight is stunning. His body is grooved and gutted and hanging in bloody shreds, yet the picture is magnetic. It draws with an unseen force. It tugs the human soul. It melts the hardest hearts.

It tells the story of a God with a love so deep that He was willing to be impaled like a lamb on a cross. It tells of a Son who humbled Himself to drink the Father's cup and pour out streams of mercy on you.

The Wound in His Heart

Narrow your vision even more now and focus again on His heart. Do you see it?

There it is.... a *Father wound!*

Yes, Jesus carries a hole like yours, carved in His heart by the abandonment of His Father.

You see, Jesus was wounded in His hands and head and back and feet and side, but the most precious wound of all is the wound in His heart. That Father wound was chiseled into His heart, etched forever on His soul. It tells you that He knows how you feel. It's a mystery now unveiled. It's a revelation of His deep love, for this wound was dug out for *you.*

Look closely at that wound now and you'll see another mystery revealed. When the soldier drove a spear into Jesus' side, blood and water streamed out. The blood signified cleansing for sin, but the water represented the river of God. For this was the pent-up river which had been treasured in the heart of Christ since the closing of the Garden of Eden.

You see, rich treasures must be mined. In Christ are hidden all *"the unending (boundless, fathomless, incalculable, and exhaustless) riches"* of Christ (Ephesians 3:8, AMP). This treasure was dug open in the earthen vessel of Jesus' heart. When the soldier's spear pierced the lining of His heart, it struck a rich vein and out rolled a river.

Just as Moses struck the rock and water flowed out, the Rock Himself had been struck and a river of life poured out. The full flood would not come until after the resurrection, but this was indeed the first release of *Rivers of Glory.*

We illustrated this one night as our revival team ministered to a little mission of broken men and women in a Christian drug rehab program. I talked with them about the cup that Jesus drank, causing a river to spill from His heart. Then I held up a glass pitcher filled with water. "His heart was like this pitcher, containing the river of God," I said.

I read this scripture: *"For he will come like a pent-up flood that the breath of the LORD drives along"* (Isaiah 59:19). Then I lifted up the glass pitcher and began pounding it with a hammer. "But it wasn't the whip that released this pent-up flood. It wasn't the thorns or nails or spear."

Still hammering the pitcher, I raised my voice and cried, "It wasn't just our sin which ravaged His soul. It was when the Father abandoned Him, poured His punishment upon Him, and He cried, *'My God, why have You forsaken Me?'* That's what broke open His heart and released the pent-up river!"

I took the hammer and smashed the vase as I held it. I cried, "When the wrath of His Father bore down upon Him, His heart burst open and He poured out the first small trickle of the river of God!" As I slammed the hammer into the vase, the glass broke and shattered, spilling the water on the floor.

One time I was giving this same illustration when a sliver of glass cut my finger. My blood mingled with the water, adding power to the illustration. I held up a bloody piece of glass, and said, "Jesus was broken so His blood for cleansing and His waters for revival could come and heal your wounded hearts!"

Now, at this mission, I showed a clip from *The Passion of the Christ* video in which Jesus' side was pierced with the spear. Out sprayed volumes of blood and water, sprinkling the centurion's face and driving him to his knees.

"That was the first release of the river!" I shouted, emotion rising in my heart. "Now God wants you to come to the river and drink! Many of you have probably been drunk on alcohol, but this river will make you drunk on God!" (see Acts 2:1-13).

We formed two lines for a river tunnel and the room erupted in glory. Men and women of all ages walked through the tunnel. One young woman, who had attempted suicide because of the death of her baby, fell to the floor, pouring out her grief. I bent over and whispered, "Honey, cry it all out." She wept and sobbed and screamed until the tears finally dried. Then the Lord showed her a vision of her baby in the arms of Jesus. Peace flooded over her and in moments she overflowed in holy laughter. She laughed and laughed, and when she tried to walk she toppled over, completely drunk in the Lord. It was wonderfully refreshing, filling her with hope and giving her a purpose to live.

As the river tunnel continued, all I could do was stand back and worship, for I knew this river was flowing because of His pierced-open heart.

The Piercing

Twenty years ago, the Lord pierced my heart with a deeper understanding of the Lamb. As I studied the cup of wrath Jesus drank, everything within me trembled and burned for the cross. It shattered my heart and released a passion like I had never known before.

This trembling has never left me. For two decades I've preached and taught and written books on the cup. Here at our camp and in my classes I've poured this message out to hundreds of students, young and old. Dozens of them have said what Sun-Hee, a Korean-American student told me, "Dr. Sandy, something has happened inside me. I feel like my heart has been pierced for the Lamb."

Some young people were visiting our camp one day when I read to them some chapters on the cup from my *Glory of the Lamb* book. Soon it became difficult to read above the sound of weeping. By the time I finished chapters four and five, most of them were on the floor sobbing.

David, a seventeen-year-old, rolled on the carpet, crying, "Jesus, You took my punishment! You drank the cup for me!" It was as though a tiny drop from the pain Jesus experienced had fallen on his heart. Later he said, "It felt like something reached into my heart and pierced it!"

One night at our camp, Margot, a Messianic Jewish girl with a powerful preaching gift, said, "Dr. Sandy, I hear students talking about having their hearts pierced by the Lord by gazing at the cup, but God has never done that in my heart. I think it's because people always tell me, 'It's not about the cross; it's all about the resurrection.'"[1]

I said, "Margot, just tell Jesus you're sorry you've neglected the cup and the cross...." She bowed her heart and began repenting to the Lord. Suddenly she doubled over, then fell to the floor sobbing. For almost an hour she wept before the Lord. She told me later, "Something happened to my heart. It was like a sword cut my heart and broke me for the Lamb!" From that time on, Margot has flowed in a river of passion and anointing that she never had before.

I received a call from Pastors Chris and Susan Clay, who pastor a church in England. They had just returned from a mission to the Ukraine where they preached about the Father's cup, urging the people not to waste one drop of the cup. The next day, a lady ran up, tears streaming down her face. "When I heard about the cup of wrath Jesus drank," she bubbled in fast Russian language, "I felt as if a sword had cut my heart in half and I felt the pain all night!"

One Sunday morning, we were lifting up the Lamb in a

church in Rotherham, England. Suddenly, the pastor's son, Nathan Morris,[2] clutched his chest and began to groan. It was as though God was sovereignly circumcising his heart (see Romans 2:29). A few months later, in Dorchester, several of my students were sharing how their hearts had been pierced. As we began praying, Pastor Peter Rooke fell to the floor, gripping his heart. He later told me, "It was like God reached in, cut my heart open, and poured in a passion for the Lamb."

What brings this piercing? Above all, the incision comes as we gaze at the cup of wrath. Try it.... Look into the contents of this cup until you can almost feel a little drop of what Jesus felt.

Slip to the floor and let the gaze of your heart behold the depths of what He did for you. See infinite wrath boiling down on the blameless One. Watch waves of eternal judgment against your sin crashing down on Jesus. Gaze into that cup until you can almost feel a tiny drop of what He suffered. Watch Him open wide and drink in every drop of that cup of wrath for you. Look at Him hanging there, paralyzed in horror by the hell He takes for you. Look into those flames, blazing down on Him. He can barely breathe. He cannot think. Words fail Him for the agony is too deep to speak.

There He hangs, utterly abandoned by God His Father. Finally, He screams up in His Father's face, *"My God, why have You forsaken Me?"*

Think what this does to the Father. He has watched His Son consuming His own wrath. He hasn't just observed it; He's the One who barreled it down on His innocent Son. This is the One He loves above all others. His own heart trembles with grief as He watches His Beloved suffer.

No wonder Mel Gibson showed us a massive tear rolling down from the Father's eyes, striking the earth and causing it to erupt in an earthquake.[3] For all of Heaven looks on in shock. Angels weep. Seraphim hide their faces from the shame. Every heart stands still. This is the eternal Son who was with His Father in the divine union of the triune Godhead throughout eternal existence.

Now the cry of Jesus rips through the heavenlies and stabs the Father's heart. His own heart breaks. The cry of His Son etches a deep wound in the heart of God.

Think about it…. Don't let this pass you by as it has so many in the Church today. Don't let this cup go to waste. Please don't squander one drop of this gruesome cup. Let it go in deep.

Fall on your face and meditate on it until something happens to you. Until you can enter into *"the fellowship of sharing in his sufferings"* (Philippians 3:10).[4] Look at His pain from drinking the Father's cup until your heart is circumcised, a veil is stripped away, and at last you can really see. Feel His agony until your heart is crucified with Christ. Until it is forever marked for God's Lamb.

It's like what the old prophet in the Temple said to the

mother of Jesus: *"A sword will pierce your own soul too"* (Luke 2:35). A sword pierced Mary's soul as she looked up at her Son, bleeding like a Lamb on the cross. But she is a picture of the Church, whose heart will be pierced as she beholds the bleeding Lamb of God. Then the veil that blinds the Church to the power and glory of the cross will be stripped away.[5]

It's just as Charles Spurgeon said, "We see the Lord pierced, and the piercing of our own heart begins."[6] Nothing pierces so deeply as looking upon the Pierced One: *"They will look on me, the one they have pierced, and they will mourn"* (Zechariah 12:10). If you will look until your heart is cleft open, a passion for the Lamb will consume you, and out of your innermost being will flow rivers of passion for Jesus.

One night Mary preached to a young-adult group in Bath, England. The people were overwhelmed by the passion that poured from her heart. She talked about the cup, the cry, the passion of her life with such intensity that people began weeping. One lady said, "Mary, the passion that's in you exploded and touched off passion in us!"

You see, once your heart has been pierced, the Gospel will burn from your lips with rivers of passion flowing through your words. That's why, when Peter preached about the Lamb at Pentecost, the people were *"cut to the heart"* (Acts 2:37).

Never have I seen this so clearly as the night I watched

twenty-one -year-old Victor Hernandez preach his first crusade in Mexico. Before thousands of Mexican people, Victor unsheathed the sword that had pierced his own heart and drove it into the hearts of the people.

"Jesus saw you as He looked down from Heaven.... He saw you burning in hell for your sin. But He came down to take the curse of your pornography, your sexual sin, your drug and alcohol addiction!"

People sat breathless, his words penetrating their hearts. "He became your substitute! He took your hell on the cross. He stood in your place and took the wrath of God against sin for you.... For *you!*"

I could almost feel his words piercing them as Victor skillfully wielded the sword and plunged it into their hearts. The crowd burst into applause and hundreds came forward for salvation, never before having heard such a clear, powerful, authoritative Gospel message.

One night at our camp, several of my students asked if they could preach their Homiletics sermon for a group of us. Katie's sermon drove us all to our knees. "Jesus calls you to come to the river and drink," she started out sweetly. "But the only reason you can drink from this river is because He drank the Father's cup!" Her voice rose, vibrating with passion as she spoke. "So look with me into the Garden of Gethsemane. Can you see Him there, writhing on the ground in bloody sweat?"

With gripping emotion she described Jesus' prayer to

the Father, as He pleaded with Him to remove the cup of wrath. She concluded by urging us to preach the power of the cross and the depths of the cup Jesus drank for us. I sat there feeling as though my heart would split in two. Like hot blades laying open our hearts, her words cut away all defenses. We all began to cry out to God in gales of intercession for your generation.

"O God, raise up a generation whose hearts bleed for Your sacrifice! Tear the veil of spiritual blindness off the Church and use these passionate students to cut through the darkness! Please, God, for the sake of Your Son, pierce the hearts of a generation with the Passion of the Lamb!"

Isaac, a young man with a powerful prophetic gift, came over to me and knelt down. "Dr. Sandy, I make a covenant with you that for the rest of my life I will preach the cup, the cross, the revelation of the Lamb!"

At last I could see that God is reaching down and piercing open young hearts with a revelation of Jesus that will change the face of Western Christianity. It's the heart of the Gospel of Christ, which will strip off the veil of blind materialism, legalism, and religion in the Church. It's a truth that will release *Rivers of Glory* to the wounds of a fatherless generation.

You see, God wants to wipe away every scar on your heart, leaving only one. He wants to pierce your heart for the Lamb of God.

So bow before the Lord once more. If you can mean this with all your heart, cry out to Him:

Holy Spirit, come.... Wipe away all my old scars and mark me with only one. Take the sword in the mouth of the Lord (see Revelation 1:16) and drive it into my heart. Let the blade go in deep. Let the point penetrate to the quick of my soul. Cut away every fleshly desire until my heart bleeds only for the Lamb. Then through my own pierced heart let your *Rivers of Glory* flow to a wounded generation.

Endnotes

1. The cross is where the work was done, and the resurrection is God's proof to humanity of the power of the cross. Both are crucial and neither should be overlooked, but for decades the cross has been severely neglected from modern and postmodern pulpits.

2. Nathan Morris is a revivalist to England. His parents, Peter and Pam Morris, pastor a revived Pentecostal church in Rotherham, where Nathan leads revival services on Saturday nights. God is using Nathan and his team to spread revival through all of England.

3. In Mel Gibson's *The Passion of the Christ* movie.

4. The verse says, "I want to know Christ and the power of his resurrection and the *fellowship of sharing in his sufferings*, becoming like him in his death" (Philippians 3:10). The Greek for *fellowship of sharing* is *koinônia*, which means, " to share in or participate in."

5. Just as Simeon said, *"The hearts of many"* will *"be revealed."* The Greek for *revealed* is *apokalupto*, meaning, "removing a veil." Yes, when at last the hearts of God's people are pierced by His sacrifice, the veil that covers the soul of the Church will be removed.

6. Charles H. Spurgeon, "How Hearts Are Softened," *Spurgeon's Expository Encyclopedia*, Vol. 8 (Grand Rapids: Baker Book House, 1977), p. 170.

Six

Rivers of Glory
The Glory Generation

John's heart pounds in his throat as he remembers the blood and water, flowing from Jesus' ruptured side. "How amazing, Lord," he whispers. "Cherubim with flaming swords guarded the entrance to the Garden of Eden where the river of life flowed in four tributaries. Now that river of life has been released from Your side, by the piercing of a soldier's sword."

John's heart warms now as he thinks of that beautiful day when the river issued more fully from Jesus' heart.

Let's go with John now to that garden tomb to see *Rivers of Glory* released from the broken Bottle....

The Resurrection Glory Erupts

Darkness still blankets the land. The body of Jesus lies silently in the rock-hewn grave. The guards sleep. But holy electricity charges the atmosphere, for another divine eruption is about to occur.

Suddenly, the glory of the Godhead descends into the garden. The essence of the Father, the Son, and the Holy Spirit pierces through the rock and penetrates the corpse laid out on the stone.

The life of God flows through His body. Jesus' takes a breath. His eyes flutter open.... Now the resurrection power of God bursts from His wounded heart. Jesus sits up and the glory of God floods the whole tomb.

Paul describes this glory as *"the power outflowing from His resurrection"* (Philippians 3:10, AMP), for now the pent-up river of God is released. This is still not the full release of these waters of life, for Jesus has not yet been glorified (see John 7:39). Even so, the resurrection glory has such ripple effects underground that *"the bodies of many holy people who had died were raised to life"* (Matthew 27:52).

Now forty days later, Jesus ascends into Heaven and sits down upon the throne. At last, He is reunited with His Father, and the pain in Their hearts can heal. But the scars don't disappear. The wounds still remain open, visible to those in Heaven. Watch now as Jesus is glorified.

Slowly He lifts His arms and the glory within Him floods out through the limitless realms of Eternity. Now at last the pent-up river of glory is released from the heart of the Lamb.

As He raises His arms, glory spills from every wound. Like a fountain of glory, streams of light shine more brightly than the rays of a trillion suns. It's a glory that shines down now to this earth, for God is releasing *Rivers of Glory* to a wounded generation.

Glory of the Son

Look now at the Source of the river—the Lamb of God Himself. See the One whose eyes flame with fire, yet once dripped tears of sorrow. See the One who wears a cloak of glory, yet once cloaked Himself in bloody human rags. See the head now circled with light, once encircled with jutting thorns.

See the One whose face glows like a morning sunrise, yet once was swollen and bruised and raw from ripped-out beard. See the mouth, filled with a golden sword, which once thirsted for a drink from engulfing the Father's cup. Hear the voice that shrieked of forsakenness, now resounding through Eternity like mighty, rushing waters (see Revelation 1:12-16).

See the Son who lived in eternal glory before the creation of the world. See the splendor beaming out from Him, for *"the Son is the radiance of God's glory"* (Hebrews 1:3). This is a radiance which no angel or heavenly being possesses. Only Jesus, along with Father and Holy Spirit, carries this innate glory.[1]

As you gaze on His divine glory, see His attributes of mercy and grace and love, pouring out through Heaven, like rays of sunlight from the center of a glowing orb. John said, *"The city does not need the sun or the moon to shine on it, for the glory of God gives it light, and the Lamb is its LAMP"*

(Revelation 21:23). He is the Sun of Righteousness, the bright Morning Star, the glorious lamp of all Heaven.

Yes, He is the source of the light that floods through Eternity. Long ago God said, *"Let there be light"* (Genesis 1:3), and the glory of the Son flooded out through time and space. Now the Son has returned to His Father and His glory floods all in all.

He revealed His glory all through the Old Testament. Moses and David and Solomon saw Him clothed in a shekinah cloud. Isaiah beheld Him on the throne with the train of His robe of glory filling the whole Temple (see Isaiah 6:1). Ezekiel saw Him looking *"like glowing metal, as if full of fire,"* from the waist up and from waist down, *Looking "like fire; and brilliant light surrounded Him"* (see Ezekiel 1:27).

Daniel saw *"his face like lightning, his eyes like flaming torches, his arms and legs like the gleam of burnished bronze, and his voice like the sound of a multitude"* (Daniel 10:6). Habakkuk said, *"His splendor was like the sunrise; rays flashed from his hand, where his power was hidden"* (Habakkuk 3:4). Malachi saw Him as the *"Sun of Righteousness,"* rising with *"healing in His wings* and *His beams"* (Malachi 4:2, AMP).

Three disciples saw Him on the Mount of Transfiguration: *"His face shone like the sun, and his clothes became as white as the light"* (Matthew 17:2). Paul saw *"the light of the knowledge of the glory of God"* shining *"in the face of* [Jesus] *Christ"* (2 Corinthians 4:6). But John saw Him as *"a Lamb, looking as if it had been slain"* (Revelation 5:6).

So let your eyes behold the Lamb of God, *"standing in the center of the throne"* (Revelation 5:6). Hear all of Heaven resounding with worship, crying out, *"Worthy is the Lamb, who was slain"* (Revelation 5:12).

Why is He so worthy? Their song explains: *"Because you were slain, and with your blood you purchased men for God from every tribe and language and people and nation"* (Revelation 5:9).

Hear hundreds of thousands of angels singing, *"Worthy is the Lamb, who was slain, to receive power and wealth and wisdom and strength and honor and glory and praise!"* (Revelation 5:12). This is the sound of Heaven which fills Eternity with worship to the Lamb. [2]

Throne Room Scenes on Earth

When the Lord wants to do something new on earth, He works through generations.[3] He has chosen your generation to bring His glory to this earth even as it is in Heaven. Of course, anyone with a childlike heart can come into this glory, but, because of your thirsty, empty hearts, the river is especially pouring down on a fatherless generation.

So look up through the window of John's Revelation to see the throne room scenes above. These glimpses of the Kingdom in Heaven show us what He wants to bring on earth. It's just like Jesus said we should pray: *"Your kingdom come, your will be done on earth as it is in heaven"* (Matthew 6:10).

He wants the Lamb to be the center of the Church, even as He is *"in the center of the throne"* in Heaven (Revelation 5:6). He wants the sound of Heaven to fill the Church, even as it fills the courts above. He wants the Lamb of God to be the focus of our worship, even as He is the focus of worship in Heaven (Revelation 5:6, 9, 11).

He wants to bring in the Feast of Tabernacles, with people of *"every nation, tribe, people, and language"* rejoicing and waving palm branches before the Lamb (7:9). He wants to tabernacle over them with His glory as He leads His people to *"springs of living water"* and wipes *"away every tear from their eyes"* (7:15, 17).

He wants to see His people overcome Satan *"by the blood of the Lamb and by the word of their testimony,"* loving not *"their lives so much as to shrink from death"* (12:11). He wants His people to *"follow the Lamb wherever he goes"* (14:4).

You say, but aren't these throne room scenes for some far-off day in the future? *No!* This is what the Lord shows us is happening in Heaven now. Jesus wants us to pray for the glory of His Kingdom to come on earth as it is in Heaven: *"Your Kingdom come....on earth as it is in Heaven.... For yours is the Kingdom and the power and the glory forever!"*

He further prayed: *"Father, I want those you have given me to be with me where I am, and to see my glory, the glory you have given me because you loved me before the creation of the world"* (John 17:24).

You see, the Lord will cover the earth with His glory, as

the waters cover the sea (see Numbers 14:21; Psalm 108:5; Isaiah 6:3; Habakkuk 2:14). But He wants to use your generation to help accomplish this, for you are the Glory Generation.

Look again at the *"river of the water of life, as clear [lampros] as crystal," (Revelation 22:1)* flowing from the throne of God and of the Lamb. The Greek word *lampros* means, "bright, shining, splendorous, elegant." These waters glow with splendor because this is a river of glory. The Lord is calling you to come to His radiant river and drink your fill from His shining streams.

Not only this, but He wants these elegant waters to cover you as the waters cover the sea. He wants to clothe you as a bride. John saw the bride of Christ, who *"has made herself ready. Fine linen, bright [lampros] and clean, was given her to wear"* (Revelation 19:8). Again the word *lampros* is used, for this linen shines with the light of the Lamb.[4]

Rivers Flowing Today

Isaiah said, *"For he will come like a pent-up flood that the breath of the LORD drives along"* (Isaiah 59:19). Already the floods are coming. We've experienced the glory in our camp, and in Pensacola, Toronto, Abbotsford, BC, and multiple churches all over the world.[5] For the wave is rising, especially over your generation.

I saw that wave break over our revival team when we answered a call to churches in England. From the moment we started in a little church in Poringland, Heaven came down. A river swept through the place and out into the streets. The Lamb of God was our message, and He confirmed His Word with miracles, salvations, and demonstrations of power. Methodists, Anglicans, and Pentecostals wept and rejoiced in the river of God. One Anglican vicar, along with a group from her congregation, lay on the floor shaking and laughing with joy. Even after we left, the Anglicans and Pentecostals decided to meet once a month for revival services.

But the best part was what happened to the youth. Our revival team was invited to speak in several classes of religious education in the public high school. The teacher told me, "We study all the religions of the world, but we've never had anyone who actually believed in Christianity. I thought it would be a novel idea to have people who believe in Christ."

I watched with joy as our revival team told how Jesus had taken away their drugs, their sexual sin, their drinking, and filled them with a purpose and passion for God. The kids in the classrooms were dumbstruck. Some cried, some argued, but all knew they had seen something they had never seen before in their lives. Several asked, "You mean you came all the way from America to tell us about God? No one has ever told us about God!"

We invited them to a pizza party on the next night, and forty kids came. Some stood outside smoking, but twenty-four came inside, and all twenty-four of them prayed to receive Christ as their Savior. Even after we left, thirty to forty young people meet weekly in that little church in Poringland.

We went on to Dorchester, and Heaven came down even more. After several days of releasing and imparting the spirit of revival, we joined with the church to hold a river tunnel for the swelling crowd of visitors. The power of God swept through that little church, bringing hope and life to southern England.

The reason I'm telling you this is because I want you to see — God is releasing a river from Heaven and you can have it too. It rushes now with power and glory for all who will jump into the streams.

When John Wesley read about the revival in America taking place in Jonathan Edwards' ministry, faith arose in his heart. He cried out to God, "If You would do it in North America, You can do it in England as well!" A few months later, as Wesley and his friends prayed at Fetterlane, suddenly the Spirit of God descended, knocking them to the floor and causing them to cry out to God.

The same thing happened at Asbury College in Kentucky and at the Azusa Street Mission in California in 1905-1906 as God breathed from Heaven on the Welsh revival. You see, when God pours down revival in one place, He will pour it out in other places if people are hungrily crying out for Him to come. What I'm trying to tell you is this: God is breathing on your generation — *now! Rivers of Glory* are rushing down from the Lamb — *today!*

All you need to do is leap into the rising flood, for Jesus is coming *"like a pent-up flood that the breath of the LORD drives along"* (Isaiah 59:19). Rivers are converging that will become oceans, and the earth will be flooded with the glory of the Lord as the waters cover the sea.

If you don't have revival in a church in your city, go somewhere to receive an impartation and bring it back with you. He wants to use you as a vessel through whom He can flow. He wants to pour through a fatherless generation to bring the glory of the Lamb to the nations.

Yes, God has called you to lift up the Lamb and carry His glory to the whole world. This is why Satan so fears you. More than forty million in your generation have been slaughtered by abortion, and he has wiped out tens of thousands through suicide, AIDS, drunk-driving collisions, and drug overdoses.

It's like Moses' generation, when all the Hebrew baby boys were to be killed. It's like the Jesus' generation, when Romans annihilated all Jewish baby boys in Bethlehem. Satan has tried to destroy you, for he knows God has chosen you for a special plan: He has targeted you for world-wide revival. He has chosen you to bring the glory of the Lamb to the nations, for you are the Glory Generation.

Those who are older and have opened their hearts to the river, can now be used in this revival. Like Caleb and Joshua, you can help lead and mentor this generation if you will release all control and jump into the rushing streams.

Will you let Him use you to bring in His glory? This move of God is not about big names. It's about God using crucified followers of the Lamb. It's about nameless, faceless ones ushering in His glory.

God's Power Through Nameless Nobodies

I'll never forget the first time I saw the Lord use unknown students in a river tunnel. I was sitting in chapel at our school and the Lord said, "Watch! This is how I will spread revival throughout America and all the world!" I sat back and watched hundreds of students walk through revival glory.

Several hundred graduating students had formed two lines. They prayed over us as the rest of the student body and faculty walked slowly through the tunnel. I stood in awe, feeling the power of God sweep through the sanctuary. Students lay on the floor, flushed and shaking under the power. Many cried. Some laughed. Every response was different, but one thing was the same — they were all being touched by the raw power of God through nameless students.

Since that time, I've seen dozens of river tunnels at our camp. Always the power of God spills out and lives are miraculously changed.

That's what happened to Jeff Turner's youth group from Michigan. He came with a hunger to see his youth leaders impacted with revival. On the very first night at camp, we formed two lines in our grape arbor outside. Teenagers started out walking normally through the line.

"*More, Lord!*" our revival students cried. "*Give her your mercy!*" *Show him Your compassion!*" "*Let Your love fill her through and through!*" "*More love!*" "*More power!*" "*More fire!*" "*More glory!*"

Halfway through the tunnel, most of them couldn't walk. They had to be carried through the lines. They wept, wailed, shook, and fell to the ground. We laid them out on blankets on the camp grounds. We prayed for them every day, imparting the river of revival to them until they went home.

The day after they returned to Michigan, Jeff called me, saying, "Dr. Sandy, I'm so excited! My wife read part of your book *The Glory of the Lamb*[6] to her Sunday school class. Afterward, she began praying for the people, and in moments they were falling under the power all over the room! Then the river spilled out through the morning service, and soon the whole church was impacted."

This is why I invite you to come to our revival camp or to a place where God is pouring down revival. Come receive an impartation and bring it back to your youth or college-age group. For this anointing is transferable. You can actually receive an impartation, as Paul said, "*I long to see you so that I may impart to you some spiritual gift*" (Romans 1:11).

"When the fire is falling," said Professor Roy Fish, "get as near as you can to the flame!"[7] The apostle Paul said,

"Fan into flame the gift of God, which is in you through the laying on of my hands" (2 Timothy 1:6). This is why "fire tunnels" or river tunnels are so powerful. Through the laying on of many hands, your own fire fans into leaping flames.

But don't wait until you can come here to get in the river. Start soaking now, in the privacy of your own prayer closet. Put on some worship music and simply lean back, close your eyes, and look up with the eyes of your heart. Focus your gaze on Jesus until you can see Him as the *"Lamb, who was slain."*

Study His beautiful wounds. They gleam like gems, engraved in the flesh of the Lamb. See the glory shining from His face and flooding all of Heaven.

Let His glory fall on you. Let it come. Breathe in His presence. He breathes out; you breathe in. Again, let your whole being become like a sponge, saturated with His presence. Let Him drench every pore of your skin, every cell of your body. Let Him deluge you with His love. As the radiant streams fill you, soak and soak and soak.

Let Him cover your earthen vessel with His glory *"as the waters cover the sea,"* for you are the Glory Generation. You are chosen by God to release *Rivers of Glory* to all the nations of this earth.

Endnotes

1. The word *radiance* in Hebrews 1:3 is *apaugasma*, meaning, "the effulgence, light, or splendor emitted or issuing from a luminous body." It is used only once in the New Testament, for it refers to a

radiance which no angel or other heavenly being possesses, only Jesus (see Bible notes on this word).

2. The sound of Heaven which I'm discussing here is the Greek word *phönë*, which means, "to shine." It occurs, for example, when Saul hears a "voice (*phönë*)" from Heaven calling him (Acts 9:4); or when Jesus speaks of hearing the "sound (*phönë*)" of the wind (John 3:8). In Revelation 14:2 and 19:6, the "sound (*phönë*)" of heaven speaks of the roar of thunder and of rushing waters.

3. For example Moses' generation was cast off and a new generation entered the Promised Land (see Numbers 32:13). In Judges the Lord dealt with His people through whole generations (see Judges 2:10). Jesus predicted great suffering would come upon the wicked generation of His day. In A.D. 70, exactly forty years (the number of a generation) after He said this, Jerusalem was destroyed and thousands of Jewish people were crucified. However, don't give up hope for the older generation, because every generation has its Joshuas and Calebs who have a different spirit.

4. Though *"fine linen stands for righteous acts,"* this linen actually glows like a lamp, for Christ is her righteousness and He is the lamp of all Heaven.

5. Even my former Assembly of God church in Idalou, Texas, under Pastor Glen Swartzendruber, is experiencing waves of God's glory.

6. See my book *The Glory of the Lamb* (Hagerstown, MD: McDougal Publishing, 2004). This can be ordered by any Christian bookstore.

7. Quoted in *Revival!* John Avanti, Malcolm McDow, and Alvin Reid, eds. (Nashville, TN: Broadman and Holman Publishers, 1996), p. 62.

Seven

Drinking From the River

New Wine for the New Wineskin

....Listen.... Shhhhh..... Can you hear it?

It's coming closer. You can hear the rushing waters. You can feel the moisture in the air. You can smell the rain in the atmosphere. You can sense the power roaring down from the Father's throne. Look more closely. You can see it spilling from the heart of the Lamb, pouring down to a fatherless generation.

So come to the waters and drink. Open wide and slake your thirst. Plunge your heart beneath the streams of this cleansing flood, for this is the river of God. It's the rushing power of the Holy Spirit. This is what Jesus suffered to give you. So let the river come. Keep taking it into the depths of your being. Keep letting it drench your soul. For *Rivers of Glory* are flowing, healing the broken, refreshing the thirsty, and spreading revival through the earth.

The Power of River Tunnels

It was the last night of our ministry in Dorchester, England. All week long our team had been preaching the

Lamb and imparting revival to the church. Now, we joined with the members of the church to form one last river tunnel. The two teams went into the back room to "soak" each other in prayer, while I explained the river tunnel to the visitors.

Each of us has a river in our belly, I told the visitors, but when we join our rivers together, the power of the Spirit increases. It's like Niagara Falls, where several rivers converge to produce a powerful overflow.[1] This is why river tunnels produce so much anointing. It's a joining together of dozens of rivers, all converging in mighty Niagaras.

We could hear the roar coming from the back room where the ministry team were soaking each other in prayer. Soon the whole team was filled and overflowing with the Holy Spirit. They came back into the sanctuary bursting with the power of the Lord. They formed two lines, facing each other, as hundreds of visitors began slowly walking, then stumbling, through the tunnel.

"More, Lord!" "Pour out Your glory!" "Holy Spirit, send the fire!" It was as though a rushing, mighty river gushed out, flooding the atmosphere with glory.

Soon young and old alike wept, worshiped, prayed, or laughed for joy. Their passion was indescribable. One young man, Jonny, head of the Christian Union in the public high school, said, "This is the greatest thing I've ever experienced in my whole life. I feel like I'm on fire!"

It was just like what the late Bill Bright, founder of Campus Crusade for Christ, said: "Whenever any Christian whose heart has been ignited with the fire of Heaven comes in touch with one whose heart is hungry for God but is presently living in spiritual defeat, another fire will be ignited."[2] That's why "fire tunnels," which I call river tunnels, are so powerful. As people with a passion for God lay hands on those with hungry hearts, a like passion is ignited.

And now, as I stood watching these English people rejoicing in God's river, I could feel the Lord's deep pleasure. I know how I felt as a young mom, when my precious twin babies giggled and splashed in their bathwater. How much more it pleases God's heart to see His kids playing and rejoicing in these rivers of revival.

And though critics may question the whole concept of revival, calling it emotionalism or revivalism, we must forgive them for they don't know what they're saying. To condemn revival is to speak against God Himself. Revival is a visitation of God. Revival is His arrival. Revival is the rushing streams of *Rivers of Glory*, flowing down from the heart of the Lamb.

New Wine for a New Wineskin

The late Pope John Paul II urged a study to discover how the Church can "appeal to youths" in "soulless America."[3] Look around this sanctuary where so many teens and young adults laugh and splash in the river. See them joyously drinking the new wine of God. I've seen this same scenario hundreds of times in America. This is the answer to the pope's appeal. This is what kids "in soulless America," as well as all the nations of the earth, are thirsty to find—a real encounter with the living God. It's new wine for the wineskin of a whole generation.

All over the nation, young people party and drink, but they're destroying their bodies and minds with the aftermath of sin. Yet this river party tops anything the secular world can offer. These young people are intoxicated with God. They are inebriated with the Holy Spirit. As they put it, they are utterly toasted, wasted, wrecked, smashed, trashed in *Rivers of Glory!*

This new wine is far better than worldly wine, for it's the new wine of the Spirit. This is the opposite of worldly wine, to which one builds up a tolerance to alcohol. With new wine, the more you drink, the easier it is to get drunk. In fact, experts tell us that the worst problem on college campuses today is binge drinking. But when young revivalists binge on this new wine, their only hangover is more love, more joy, more passion for God.

In the upper room at Pentecost, the hundred and twenty exploded with so much joy and life that people mocked and said, *"They have had too much wine"* (Acts 2:13). Apparently, they acted like they were drunk because they were. They were drunk with God.

Being drunk in the Holy Spirit is nothing new. When E.

Stanley Jones, a Methodist missionary to India, was a young man at Asbury College in 1905, he was praying one night with several young men in a dorm room. He said, "Suddenly we were all swept off our feet by a visitation of the Holy Spirit.... For three or four days it could be said of us, as was said of the original Pentecost, 'They are drunk.' We were drunk with God."[4] And though some would call this simply an "experience," Jones said this encounter with God in revival was what led him into the mission field.

In fact, the reason being "drunk with God" happens more today is because God is releasing more of His new wine to the wineskin of a new generation. And believe me, He has saved the best wine for last.

Whether old or young — if you're willing to lose your dignity, your pride, and control — you can drink from this new wine too. But be forewarned — all respectability will wash away in the streams of His glory. You'll laugh until you cry because you're deliriously happy in Jesus.

And while some worry about what others might think if they fall or shake in God's presence, what does it matter? It's not people we're here to please. It's Him! I can only tell you, encountering the pure presence of God in this river of wine is the most wonderful experience on earth.

Some of you, however, may be discouraged because you really want to be "drunk in the Lord," but it never seems to happen for you. My suggestion is — don't worry about it. Just ask the Lord to give you His peace and keep on drinking from the river. Soon you'll reach your saturation point.

Doubting the Manifestations

Before I was touched by God's Spirit in the river, I criticized the manifestations of the Spirit. It offended me to see people cry out or fall on the floor shaking. But once I experienced it for myself, I knew this was real. People tend to judge another's experience with God by their own lack of experience with God.

Jonathan Edwards, considered the greatest revival theologian in American history,[5] was criticized by the famous theologian Charles Chauncy for all the "bodily effects" occurring in the revival. Chauncy described Edwards' meeting as being filled with confusion, some screaming, some praying, others singing or lying prostrate on the floor. He warned of "roarings, tremblings, and the strangest bodily effects," which "proved the work could not be of God."[6] In a classic work on revival, Edwards responded:

> *Now if such things are enthusiasm, and the fruits of a distempered brain, let my brain be evermore possessed of that happy distemper! If this be distraction, I pray God that the world of mankind may be all seized with this benign, meek, beneficent, beatific, glorious distraction![7]*

Of course, we don't seek manifestations; we seek Him. So whether one shakes or falls is irrelevant, but the way I see it is this: If God can shake mountains (see Isaiah 54:10); if He can shake the threshold of the Temple (see Isaiah 6:4); if He can shake the heavens and His voice can shake the earth (see Hebrews 12:26); and if He can shake an upper room in Jerusalem (see Acts 4:31), then it's nothing for Him to shake a human body.

That's why Scripture asks, *"Should you not tremble in my presence?"* (Jeremiah 5:22).[8] The question, however, is not whether one shakes or falls, but has one's heart been shaken by God's presence? Has one's life been changed and has fruit come forth as a result of the touch of God?

Fruit Grows by the River

Through the years, I've watched tremendous fruit produced from those who soaked in the river. But even in a Christian setting, I've seen revival students, whose hearts were pierced by the Lamb and who immersed themselves in His river, terribly mocked by other Christians.

When I think of some of the most persecuted students, who faithfully drank from the river here at our camp just nine months ago, I'm amazed at the fruit. Five of them are now pouring their lives out as missionaries in Ghana. Two are missionaries in England. Two just recently laid hands on the blind and deaf in India as they received their sight and hearing.

One of our students, Victor Hernandez, was the most persecuted of all. When pastors in Reynosa, Mexico, saw a video of him preaching and shaking under the power, they wept. "We've got to get behind this kid," they said. "He's anointed!"

He was given the largest stadium in the city, where he held a revival campaign with thousands attending. At one point, a storm blew in and it started to sprinkle. Victor stomped his feet, commanding the storm to leave, and it did. Hundreds prayed to receive Christ and dozens were healed. One lady whose hands were completely gnarled into fists told of being a witch, a murderer, and having made a pact with the devil. But when she received prayer, her hands opened up and the tumor in her breast dissolved.

A girl in a wheelchair couldn't walk, but after being soaked in prayer, she stood and took huge steps across the platform. The joy on her face was worth the whole crusade. Victor lifted his face toward Heaven, with tears streaming down his cheeks, and humbly thanked the Lord, for he knew — the only reason this crippled girl could walk was because of the costly sacrifice of the Lamb.

Victor is just like you. A few years ago he was shy and awkward in speech. But when the Lamb pierced His heart, out flowed a river of passion. And though many mocked him, he soaked and soaked in the river, for he was being prepared as a revivalist. Then he spent six months as an intern with Todd Bentley, and signs and wonders and the authority of God were released into his life. God blew open the doors of ministry, and now pastors in Mexico believe he is the revivalist who will take the nation for Christ.

This is what I call fruit, but it's fruit that grows from drinking from the river. It's like the trees in Ezekiel's vision. Month after month they bear fruit because their roots go down into the streams of the river (see Ezekiel 47:12).

When twenty-nine-year-old Todd Bentley ministered here at Brownsville, we saw, before our very eyes, several deaf people receive their hearing. One lady, who had endured eleven back surgeries, had a steel plate in her back with constant pain. Unable to bend over because of the plate, she came to the platform, pain free, and bent over to touch the floor with her fingers. The next day, x-rays showed that the steel plates had dissolved.[9]

At the end of the service on Todd's first night at Brownsville, he suddenly turned his attention to a row of students who were on our staff at camp. He hurried over and cried, *"A mighty anointing is coming to this whole row of young people."* Then he swept his hand across our row and shouted, *"Fire! Fire! Fire!"* I'm not young, but I hit the floor with the rest of them. Then Todd burst into prophecy:

> *There is a Joel's Army; there is an army of signs and wonders; there is a radical generation of firebrands and fire starters, burning and shining lamps of revival!.... There's a fresh anointing of God to young people, and swords and spears and battle weapons of the Spirit are being placed in their hands even in this place....*

Todd walked over to the youth group attending our camp and cried, *"I'm prophesying a youth revival.... Fire! Fire! Fire!"* and all the kids fell to the carpet. He continued proph-

esying, *"I'm contending to see a Joel's Army in Jesus' name!*
We prophesy it in this place: a Joel's Army, in Jesus' name!"

Now, here at our Camp America Ablaze, we're holding
"Joel's Army Boot Camps" (see flyer in back of book). Be-
ginning sometime in 2006, teens and young adults are invited to come for impartation and releasing in the river.

Listen...

Even now the river of life tumbles from God's throne,
rushing out through the courts of Heaven, coursing down
to planet earth. It splashes over mountains and spills into
valleys, seeking a riverbed to fill. It streams into the low
and thirsty places of the land, soaking into the gullies—
the carved-out places in human souls. Finally the waters
find a riverbed—the cracked-open hearts of a fatherless
generation.

You see, this is the open secret. This is the mystery of
the cross: that God would pour His cup of wrath upon His
Son until His heart ruptured open and poured out *Rivers
of Glory*. Now this river of God has come to a fatherless
generation. We who are older can jump into the streams if
we will come as little children.

This is indeed the early stages of the fulfillment of the
Feast of Tabernacles, which the Lord said was for the fatherless, the widows, and the aliens (see Deuteronomy
16:14). It's the "pouring out of waters," basking in the glory,
drinking of the wine of joy, and gathering in the harvest of
fruit. [10]

So listen once again.... Can you hear it? Can you see the moisture dancing in the air? Can you feel the warm tingle on your face or in your hands? Can you sense the electricity charging the atmosphere? It's the radiant river of God.

Come up close to the source of the river and stand beneath the raw power of the waterfall. Stand so close to the ledge of the falls, you can almost reach out and catch the waters in your hands.

Now still your heart and let that power come down on you. Let it roar through your whole being. Here beneath the rushing streams, let the sound of Heaven pulse through your head. Let the thundering waters flood your whole being. These are the *Rivers of Glory* tumbling down from the Lamb. Let the rivers come. Drink and drink and drink until you can hold no more. Then go out and spread this river to others, for rivers that don't flow out become swamps.

Remember, however, that Jesus is the source, the reservoir, the divine container of the river of God. Drink your fill from these refreshing streams, but with every touch of His power, every sip of new wine, every taste of joy, never forget—it all flows down from the wounded heart of the Lamb.

Endnotes

1. The sound of crashing waters drew the first explorers to Niagara Falls. That's why natives named it *Onguiaahra*, meaning, "great thunderer of waters" (Joan Colgan Stortz, *Niagara Falls* [Markham, Ontario: Irving Westorf and Co., Ltd. 1994], p. 2).

2. Bill Bright, quoted in John Avanti, Malcolm McDow, and Alvin Reid, eds., *Revival!* (Nashville, TN: Broadman and Holman Publishers, 1996), p. 176.

3. "Pope Worries About 'Soulless' American Life," Foxnews.com, May 28, 2004.

4. E. Stanley Jones, *Song of Ascents: A Spiritual Autobiography* (Nashville, TN: Abingdon Press, 1968), p. 68.

5. D. Martyn Lloyd-Jones said that Edwards is "preeminently the theologian of Revival, the theologian of experience, or as some have put it, 'the theologian of the heart'" (D. Martyn Lloyd-Jones, *The Puritans* [Westchester, PA: Banner of Truth Trust, 1987], p. 361).

6. Charles Chauncy, *Seasonable Thoughts on the State of Religion in New England* (Boston, MA: Rogers and Fowle, 1743), p. 6.
Interestingly, in tracing Charles Chauncy's influence in history, Ian Murray points out that Chauncy's work eventually evolved into Unitarianism and Universalism. On the other hand, the influence of Jonathan Edwards work on evangelical Christianity still inspires us today (Ian Murray, *Jonathan Edwards: A New Biography* [Edinburgh: Banner of Truth Trust, 1996], p. 454).

7. Jonathan Edwards', *The Works of Jonathan Edwards*, Vol. 1, "Thoughts on Revival" (Edinburgh: Banner of Truth Trust, 1995), p. 378.
Edwards never disapproved of bodily manifestations, though he insisted they proved nothing. In his "Thoughts on Revival," he glowingly described the experiences of people he knew who trembled, cried out, wept profusely, leapt for joy, fainted with love sickness, swooned, and were swallowed up by the glory of God like a mote in the beam of a ray of sunshine. His own beloved wife was in a trance-like state for seventeen days. Every time she heard the name Jesus she fell back into the glory.

8. Look up all the verses on *trembling* which also means, "shake or shaking," and you'll have the scriptural foundation for shaking under the power of God's presence.

9. Sometimes Todd would pray for twelve hours a day, until he actually broke through into the miraculous. He is a forerunner to your generation, showing you that you too can have signs and wonders in your ministry for Jesus. Todd leads "Miracle Festivals" all over the world, with hundreds of thousands attending and thousands of verified miracles. Blind eyes open. The deaf hear. Stroke victims rise from wheelchairs. Cripples walk. Spines heal. Cancers flee. In his book *Journey Into the Miraculous*, Todd tells about locking himself in his bedroom and praying for hours. "I was so hungry I literally felt like I was about to die if God didn't visit me. It was an unquenchable thirst." Often he would pray and soak and worship for twelve hours a day. Sometimes the Lord's presence would lift and he'd cry, "Lord, no!" He said, "I'd chase God down again and wham, I was on the floor once more" (Todd Bentley, *Journey Into the Miraculous* [Ladysmith, BC, Canada: Sound of Fire Productions Ltd., 2003], pp. 97-98).

10. At the Feast of Tabernacles the priests poured wine and water down the sides of the altar of burnt offering. Part of the fulfillment of this feast will be the outpouring of the waters of revival and the pouring out of the new wine. The feast also commemorated the cloud of glory with the lighting of the massive candelabra. It was also the feast of the ingathering of fruit, which speaks of the coming harvest of souls.

Eight

Rivers to the Lamb

Bringing Him the Reward of His Suffering

John sees again the door in Heaven swinging open. He comes on up, looking into the throne room. He enters beyond the open veil and sees the seraphim, the burning ones, hiding their faces from the brightness of His glory. He watches streams of light filling the Holy of Holies. He looks at the One from whom the glory flows, and his heart fills with worship.

Come one last time with John and gaze upon the glory of the Lamb. Feel the heat warming your heart and burning your face. Sense the power of pure holiness filling the atmosphere. Breathe it in. Every breath you take fills with glory. Let His goodness saturate every cell of your being.

This is the presence of God. This is what you've longed for all of your life. One touch of His glory ruins you. Once you've tasted, you can never be satisfied without living in His presence.

Now, with eyes of faith, watch the Father point toward His Son and thunder — *"Behold the Lamb, slain from the foundation of the world!"* See the Father's love for His Son, bursting from His heart, filling all of Heaven with the glory of His love.

The Cry of God's Heart

One night in high worship at church, the Father spoke clearly to my spirit:

> When My Beloved One suffered on the cross, My own suffering was immeasurable. But when He screamed up in My face, the cry of My Son cut a deep wound in My heart. Now there is only one thing that will soothe that wound, and it's this: TO SEE MY SON RECEIVE THE REWARD OF HIS SUFFERING.

This is the cry that aches in the Father's heart. Now He yearns to replace the cry of a fatherless generation with the cry of His heart. Will you let Him burn this cry in you? Will you dedicate your life to bringing His Son the reward He deserves?

It's like the true story of the wealthy father whose son had Down's syndrome and died, breaking the father's heart. Soon the old man died, leaving no will and no heirs to inherit his estate. An estate auction was held to sell his possessions, and at the auction sat the little housekeeper who had loved and cared for the boy until he died. Though she had very little money, she took all she had to the auction so she could buy the picture of the boy. The picture was auctioned off first, and because no one showed any interest, she bought it for a low price. Then she opened it to clean the glass and out fell some important papers — the official will of the wealthy man. The will said, "I leave all of my estate to the person who buys the picture of my son!"

The father wanted everything he owned to go to the one who loved his son. That's how God feels. He looks for those who will love Him so deeply they will want to bring His Son the reward of His suffering. He looks for those who will let Him place His cry in their hearts. His eyes search the earth to find one whose only motive for ministry is to bring Jesus His reward.

Mary wrote in a note: "My whole life has been shaken and turned upside down.... My mind has shifted and my soul has been pierced. I have the most precious thing of all. I have deep, deep inside of me a pleading cry that I know will never cease.... I long to see Jesus receiving His reward. He must receive it!"

Will you let Him plant this cry in you? Will you look upon His sacrifice until every other cry is consumed? Until every other motive burns up in the fire of the cross? Until every other passion fades?

Look upon the Pierced One until your own heart bleeds for souls. Until you are broken for the broken. Until everything within you yearns to soothe the ache in the Father's heart. Until your heart burns to bring His Son the reward of His suffering. [1]

What is that reward? First, it's telling the world what Jesus did for them. It's causing the lost to see the cup of wrath, which Jesus endured for them. Then it's bringing those souls to the Lamb.

Furthermore, it's pouring out God's love to homeless orphans. It's ministering to the sick. It's giving food to poor, discarded people, for when you do, you'll be feeding Jesus. Just as He said: *"Whatever you did for one of the least of these brothers of mine, you did for me"* (Matthew 25:40). This is a purpose for which you could die; it will cause you to really live.

Will you let Him carve this cry in you? If you will, no longer will you be filled with a cry of pain. Though tears of grief once soaked your pillow, now tears of passion will soak the altar of prayer. Like Elijah drenching the altar with water, now you will drench the altar with tears for lost souls.

"I was praying last night," cried Victor. "Oh, Dr. Sandy, I could see the lost, dark and dead, falling into hell! I could feel the heart of God, sorrowing over them. I could sense His deep sadness for souls, until I was moaning with God's grief for the lost. I wept and prayed until I was worn out, and then I lay in His presence for hours, unable to even move my little finger!"

Every Saturday night Angela, Michelle, and dozens of young men and women hit the streets of Pensacola, preaching until their throats are raw. Angela cries to the drunks at the beach: "Behold the Lamb of God! He took your sin and pain! He took your punishment, so He could give you purpose!" Angela has been mocked again and again, but she doesn't care. She's driven by love. She must bring Jesus the reward of His suffering.

Trevor and Josh have been pouring their lives out in Ghana, and as they have lifted up the Lamb, people have cried out, "How can we be saved?" In fact, when Josh came home from Ghana, doctors discovered he had the worst case of cerebral malaria they had ever seen. Just before slipping into a coma, he moaned, "I've got to get out of this bed and get back to Ghana!" When he came out of the coma, which doctors said had to be the hand of God, he said again, "I've got to get back to Ghana!" Why was he so willing to pour his life out, even to the point of death? Because he burns to bring Jesus the reward of His sacrifice.

In Mexico, before Victor's crusade, he led his team to the city dumps, where people live in squalor with no running water and very little food. The crowds never saw his team ministering to the people in the dumps and giving food which would last for weeks. But God saw and He was pleased, for they were bringing His Son the reward He deserves for what He has done for them.

With millions of orphans living on the streets of this world,[2] others plan to rescue dying street orphans, bringing them to the Lamb, and raising them up to be an army of young revivalists. With this same dream in her heart,

Mary said with conviction, "I don't want life to pass me by. With the short life I have on earth, I want to bring Jesus the reward of His suffering!"

These young ministers are a new breed, not caught up with selfish ambition and materialism. They care nothing about climbing corporate ladders in the world or political ladders in the church. They would rather live in the streets to give cups of living water to hurting people than live in a palace and do nothing for the One who bled for them.

They are like the young lady who was seen by some American businessmen, wiping the sores of a leper in India. One of the men snorted, "I wouldn't do that for a million dollars!" She looked up with a smile as bright as a sunrise and said, "Neither would I, but I would do it for Jesus Christ!"

The Cry of a John the Baptist Generation

Your generation is like John the Baptist, standing in the streams of a river, pointing at Jesus and crying, *"Behold the Lamb of God who takes away the sin of the world!"* This was his grandest message, his finest sermon. His highest calling, above all others, was to point the way to the Lamb.[3]

You are a John the Baptist Generation, and like John, standing in the river, your highest call is to point to the source of the river and cry, *"Behold the Lamb of God!"* Once your heart has been pierced for the Lamb, everything within you will want to bring glory to Him for what He suffered for you.

You see, God has been waiting for your generation to come of age. He's been waiting for a young John the Baptist Generation to arise and explode across this earth, crying in the wilderness of this world— *"Behold the Lamb of God!"* For this has been the forgotten message of today's Church. Though Paul resolved to preach only *"Jesus Christ and him crucified"* (1 Corinthians 2:2), rarely do we hear the Lamb preached with power today.

Like Isaac asked his father, your generation still asks, *"Father, where's the Lamb?"* (see Genesis 22:7). Why hasn't anyone ever told us?[4] In fact, Mel Gibson told of a young lady who drove home after seeing *The Passion of the Christ*, praying, "I'm sorry, Lord.... I *forgot*."[5] The reason she forgot is because we—my generation—forgot to tell her.

Because we forgot to reveal the cup of wrath, a whole generation doesn't understand the depths of the cross. When nineteen-year-old Holly visited our camp, she overheard students talking about the cup. "What is this cup?" she asked. I handed her a term paper from Sandy, one of my students. She read it and was undone. A few weeks later she preached in her church: "I've been to church all my life," she said with fire in her eyes. "But no one has ever told me about the cup of wrath Jesus drank on the cross! Why not? How could something so crucial be so overlooked?"

Holly's insightful question challenges the Church today. It's like the story of the young missionary who asked the girl he loved to marry him in a letter. He wrote, "If I don't hear from you, I'll know you have turned me down." The young lady eagerly responded with a letter, accepting his proposal. She handed the letter to her brother to take to the post office, but years passed and she never heard from the man she loved. One day, she was cleaning out her brother's closet and found an old yellowed letter, folded in a pocket of her brother's jacket. He had forgotten to mail the letter.

Oh, please—you who are reading these pages— don't forget to tell about the Lamb! Please don't let another century pass without telling people about the depths of His suffering. Don't let another generation slip into hell without telling them about a Son who drank the Father's cup of wrath and took their punishment of hell. Don't let another lifetime pass without bringing Him the reward of His suffering.

In the Middle East, Muslims crowded the theaters to see *The Passion of the Christ* movie, hearing it was "anti-Semitic." Missionaries reported "hearing sobs and gasps from the audience as they saw Jesus flogged and crucified."[6] After the movie, questions poured from these Muslims: "Why did Jesus do it?" "Why did the tear fall from Heaven down to earth?" "Why did the devil scream when Jesus died?"

Who will answer these questions? Will you? Will you spend your life bringing the Lamb of God out of the shadows? Will you bring Him His reward?

With Muslims and Jews, don't use the term *the cross.* Though it is biblical, the cross was the symbol for the Crusades, in which thousands of Muslim and Jewish people were slaughtered. Even Hitler used a bent cross as his symbol during the Holocaust. Do, however, tell them about *the Lamb!* The entire history of the Jewish race is splattered with the blood of lambs. So tell them about blood dripping, tears flowing, whips thrashing. Tell them about the Son of God who was skinned, flayed like a lamb for the morning sacrifice.[7]

Tell everyone what He did, but tell them graphically. Please don't let the creative expression end with Mel Gibson. Use your own creative abilities to tell the story over and over again. Through art and music and writing and drama and movies and videos and dance and preaching — or whatever creative talents you have — show them the Lamb.

It's the seeing that breaks them: *"They will LOOK ON ME, the one they have pierced, and they will mourn"* (Zechariah 12:10). The world still waits for a Gospel that cuts to the heart. That's why they need to *see* what you are saying. They need to have their ears turned into eyes until they *feel* it in their gut.

So cause them to see with the eyes of their hearts. Let them see thorns piercing, nails pounding, sword plunging, wrath burning, and love consuming. Through everything you do and say, let them see the Lamb.

This has always been the Father's desire. Above all, He wants to unveil to the world the beauty of His Son as the Lamb. God closed the Bible with the book of Revelation, which is a revelation of His Son as the Lamb. In the same way He will close this age by unveiling His Son as the Lamb. And from this simple but burning truth will flow *Rivers of Glory to a Fatherless Generation* and all the generations to come.

The Fruit of His Suffering

Lately I've been weeping a lot as I've seen Jesus receive His reward through a young generation. When David returned home from our camp, after being broken by the cup (see chapter 5), he started a Christian club in his secular high school which he called "Fill the Void." He phoned me to say that over fifty kids were coming and most of them had already gotten saved in the club.

One day Tanya, a student from Mexico, ran up to me and cried, "Oh, Dr. Sandy, I was preaching to eight hundred teenagers at a conference in Mexico during the holidays. But when I told them about the cup of wrath, they began to weep and groan. Some even fell on their faces, screaming over the suffering of Jesus when He drank the Father's cup. They were cut open with the cross of Jesus!"

Margot called me, overflowing with excitement, as she told how she had preached the cross and the cup at a summer camp. The youth were so broken by the cup that they filled the altars, giving their lives to God. John, a young prophet on our team, heard the word of the Lord and ushered the healing river of the Lamb into the sanctuary in England. The power outflowing from the cross brought amazing healings in our midst.

One night we sat around a campfire at our camp, roasting hot dogs with a Michigan youth group. When the kids started talking about the cross, my ears perked up. I asked what Jeff, a former student of mine and now their youth pastor, had been teaching them. They told me all about the cup, the wrath of God, the ruptured heart of Jesus.

I asked them to speak in my New Testament class the next day. And my students sat slack-jawed as these teenagers expounded a theology that excels most theologians. One girl, Megan, fell on her knees and cried, "Please preach the cross to my generation! Please! Nothing else can reach us! You've got to tell us what Jesus did on the cross!"

Recently, as Hurricane Katrina roared in upon the Gulf Coast, we took a youth group, here from California, to the hurricane shelter. Even as the storm blew in, the Holy Spirit fell upon the kids and they hit the floor shaking and crying out to God. When we got back to the camp, we tried to have a prayer tunnel, but the power fell so strongly we couldn't even get them into the tunnel.

On their way back to California, they all started saying, "We must give this revival fire away to our church." Frank, an eighteen-year-old, said wisely, "Yes, but remember, we must tell them all about the Lamb!" When I heard about this, all I could do was close my eyes and whisper, "Jesus, here is Your reward!"

The Harvest by the River

Now it's time for you. God wants to use you as a young revivalist to your generation. He wants to pierce your heart for the Lamb until rivers of revival fire stream from within you. He wants the fire to blaze so brightly from within you that others will want to draw near to feel the heat and watch you burn.

As you step out with the message of the Lamb piercing your soul, the fire of holiness blazing in your eyes, a passion for souls surging in your spirit, compassion for the poor melting your heart, and *Rivers of Glory* rushing from your belly — you will be like the Olympic runner who touches the torch to the cauldron of oil, causing it to burst into flames.

God will use you to touch the cauldron of oil inside your generation, causing the fatherless to burst into flames of love for the Lamb. And though some will mock, many will fall on their faces when they finally see what Jesus did for them.

You see, wherever the river flows, fruit grows and huge nets gather fish for God (see Ezekiel 47:9-12). Indeed, as you live your life in the river, you'll be used by Him in a massive end-time harvest of souls for the Lamb. [8]

But you'll take no credit for yourself, for you have felt His tears splash upon your heart. You have touched His warm blood washing over your wounds. You have drunk deeply from His river and tasted of the glory streaming down from His heart. Your own heart has been forever healed by His waters, pierced by His Passion, and filled with *Rivers of Glory.*

Now all you can do is fall on your knees, lift your hands, and look into His eyes. With trembling heart, you will cry — *Lamb of God, here is Your reward!"*

You will pour these rivers back on Him, for rivers always seek to flow back to their source in the ocean. This river flows from Him and through Him and back to Him, bringing Jesus the reward He deserves.

Even now, as you lay this book aside, won't you bend to your knees and cry to the Lord:

> Jesus, forgive me for placing other desires in front of Your sacrifice. Help me never to waste one drop of the cup You drank for me. Holy Spirit, burn a passion for the Lamb in me until every other passion fades. Consume every other motive, every other desire of my life. Father, let me touch the wound in Your heart by bringing Your Son the reward He deserves. For the rest of my life, I will live to bring the Lamb the reward of His suffering bringing *Rivers of Glory* to a wounded generation!

Endnotes

1. Under Ludwig von Zinzendorf, the Moravians adopted this heart-cry hundreds of years ago. "May the Lamb receive His due reward for what He suffered on the cross!" was their motto. Read this story in my book *The Glory of the Lamb.*

2. According to the United Nations, there are over three billion children under the age of fifteen; of these, two billion live in extreme poverty and are malnourished. Seventeen million children die of starvation each year. One hundred million children live on the streets. In 2001 there were thirteen million AIDS orphans. Ten million children are exploited in the sex industry. On average, many child prostitutes turn over thirty "tricks" a day. In the last ten years, 60 to 100 million girls are "missing" from the world's population (from "United Nations State of the World's Children 2002," cited in Eric D. Frans, *On the Fragile Feel of Children* [Kelowna, BC, Canada: Hope for the Nations] 2002).

3. Charles Spurgeon said, "The preacher's principal business, I think I might say his only business, is to cry, 'Behold the Lamb of God!' For this reason was John born and sent into the world" (Charles H. Spurgeon, "Behold the Lamb!" *Spurgeon's Expository Encyclopedia,* Vol. 3 [Grand Rapids, MI: Baker Book House, 1977], p. 103).

4. I want to give credit to Jamie Clay who received this revelation about the Lamb for your generation while visiting here from England.

5. *Outreach* Magazine, *Vol. 3:1,* (January/February, 2004), p. 45.

6. "Muslims Respond to *The Passion of the Christ, Spread the Fire* Magazine, Issue 3, p. 22.

7. The message of the cross has not only been forgotten; it's also been distorted. It has been used as a symbol for the Crusades, when thousands of Jews and Muslims were slaughtered. Even Hitler used a bent cross for his swastika as he systematically annihilated six million Jews, saying he was doing it for Christ.

8. A massive harvest of souls is coming. It is the fulfillment of the Feast of Tabernacles as the harvest of the fruit is gathered. It's the fulfillment of Ezekiel's river vision as huge amounts of fish are caught. It's the fulfillment of prophecy as the earth is filled with the glory of the Lord.

Glory of the Lamb Internships

September 1 - December 1, 2006

The Glory
of the Lamb

Before going into your ministry or off to university or college, take 3 months as Dr. Sandy and her staff pour into you every day at Camp America Ablaze (on Gulf Coast).

What you can expect from this internship:
- Your wounds healed in the Father's love
- Your heart pierced by a revelation of Jesus as the Lamb
- Deep encounters with the Holy Spirit
- Impartations of Revival Fire
- Training in prophetic and healing evangelism
- Rich insights into the Bible with Dr. Sandy
- Ministry opportunities

Discover how you can bring Jesus the reward of His suffering through your short life on earth.

email: campablaze@juno.com or drsandy7@yahoo.com
phone: 251.962.7172

Revival Camps

Youth pastors, bring your youth or young adults to **Camp America Ablaze** *where hundreds of youth are being ignited with revival fires, bringing it back to their churches. Pastors, bring your leaders for a weekend of refreshing and impartations of revival to spread to your whole church.*

Lighted tennis court, basketball court, sand volleyball, swimming pool, baseball, soccer, beautiful prayer garden for meetings under the trees, use of kitchen and grills for meal prep, 60 beds, and most of all — *impartations of REVIVAL FIRE!*

Cost: $25 a person per night
(prices subject to change)
e-mail: campablaze@juno.com
or drsandy7@yahoo.com
phone: Dr. Sandy at (251) 962-7172

Mission Focus: *All our teaching, preaching, drama, and music focus on the cross of the Lamb. The Holy Spirit honors this focus by pouring out revival fire on hungry hearts. We yearn to bring Jesus the reward of His suffering and to impart this pure motive to a new generation.*

BOOT CAMP

Equipping a Young Generation to
Bring God's Kingdom on Earth

EQUIPPED & ACTIVATED IN...

* Holy Ghost Revival

* Signs and Wonders

* The Sword of the Cross

* Prophetic Evangelism

* Healing Evangelism

Contact: Piercedpassion.org
or Freshfire.Ca
850-291-4291

Location: Camp America Ablaze
Lillian, AL Phone 251-962-7172
email: campablaze@juno.com

Other Books by Sandy Kirk

The Glory of the Lamb
1-158158-074-6

A Revelation of the Lamb
1-158158-063-0

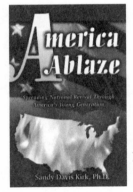

America Ablaze
1-158158-053-3

You may order these books by going to
www.mcdougalpublishing.com or calling 301.797.6637.